The Power-Filled Christian

The Work of the Holy Spirit in Man

Zondervan Publishing House
Grand Rapids, Michigan

THE POWER-FILLED CHRISTIAN
Copyright © 1984 by The Zondervan Corporation
Grand Rapids, Michigan

Clarion Classics are published by Zondervan
Publishing House, 1415 Lake Drive, S.E.,
Grand Rapids, Michigan 49506

Library of Congress Cataloging in Publication Data

The Power-Filled Christian.

    1. Holy Spirit.   2. Spiritual life.
BT121.2.P69   1984   234   84-5115
ISBN 0-310-33471-3

All passages from Scripture are taken from the King James and the
Revised Versions of the Bible. The King James Version is used
unless the reference is marked RV in parenthesis.

Printed in the United States of America

86 87 88 89 90 / 10 9 8 7 6 5 4 3 2

Contents

Author's Preface

An old puritan preacher declared that the Holy Spirit was the least *known,* the least *loved,* and the least *worshiped* of the Three Persons of the Trinity.

Yet no man can live the Christian life without the indwelling of the Holy Spirit, and none can have the "life more abundant" unless the Holy Spirit has full control.

This little volume, which speaks of the Blessed Holy Spirit's work in man, is the sixth of a series.

Each of these books is the outcome of earnest and eager inquiries from distressed souls.

They were written without any thought of unity of purpose. Yet as the author looks back he is startled to find how the Power-Full Christian is a natural and necessary sequel to the other five.

1. *How to Live the Victorious Life* spoke of the Indwelling Christ as the source and power of all victory over sin in the heart and life. But is it not the Holy Spirit who receives of the things of Christ and shows them unto us; who speaks of Christ; who guides into all truth? (John 16:13,14).

2. *He Shall Come Again* tells us of our Lord's second coming. Will that not be effected "through the Eternal Spirit"? In all the pages of Scripture there is but one recorded prayer of the Holy Spirit, who intercedes "with groanings which cannot be uttered" (Rom. 8:26). But on the last page of our Bible, when our Lord cries, "Behold, I come quickly," the Blessed Spirit finds utterance and joins with the Bride in saying "Come!" (Rev. 22:12, 17).

3. *The Happy Christian.* Our Lord's rejoicings were "in the Spirit" (Luke 10:21)—and we, too, find "joy in the Holy

Spirit" (Rom. 14:17), for "the fruit of the Spirit is . . . joy" (Gal. 5:22).

4. *The Kneeling Christian* brought us to recognize that "we know not how to pray," but that the Holy Spirit intercedes for us and in us, helping our infirmities (Rom. 8:26–27).

5. *The Glory Christian.* Christ Himself lived a radiant life in the power of the Holy Spirit. That same Holy Spirit has come to "glorify" Christ (John 16:14) to us and in us and through us.

It is the Holy Spirit Who conveys to us the glory which Christ received from the Father to give to us (John 17:22). So, then, it is a fitting thing that:

The Power-Full Christian should follow in the train of those other volumes.

May that same Blessed Holy Spirit—Comforter—Divine Instructor—Guide—Counselor—Illuminator of both the Written and the Living Word, open our minds and gain complete control of our wills so that all who read these pages may become Power-Full Christians.

1
Power From
on High

"Power from on high." That is the promise of the Father, and the promise of our Savior. Who can read those words without a thrill or without a hope?

"Tarry ye in the city of Jerusalem until ye be endued with power from on high" (Luke 24:49). Surely this command of the Lord Jesus to His disciples must have caused them great surprise and not a little excitement, coupled with eager expectation. "Not many days hence" they were to be "baptized with the Holy Ghost" (Acts 1:5).

"Ye shall receive power, after that the Holy Ghost is come upon you" (Acts 1:8). The other Comforter—that wonderful Comforter who was to convict the world of sin, and of righteousness, and of judgment—who was to teach Christ's followers "all things" and to bring all things to their remembrance; who was to guide them into all truth, was also to bring "power from on high." And as we read the Savior's promise to "his own," we feel intuitively that the promise is to us. And our hearts beat faster and our longing desire is buoyed up with expectant hope.

Power? Power from on high? Power sufficient for every need—every emergency, and for everyone?

Is not this the very thing we so greatly need? Everyone needs power, and most men covet power. And no Christian should rest content until he is filled with "power from on high."

Are not Christians everywhere praying for power? The

wide world over, whenever men and women come together for prayer, the cry goes up, "O Lord, send the power." "O God, fill us with the Holy Spirit and with power." Yet is it not a fact that somehow or other this "power from on high" seems to come but very rarely in answer to our cry? How often has the power, evident power, come down upon any prayer meeting attended by you? We do not mean excitement, or shouting, or ecstasy, but deep, spiritual power?

What is this "power from on high" that we seek? Is it not true that very few believers really know what they are asking for when they seek power? How many of us have ever knelt in silence before God with our Bibles open before us, to endeavor to find out just what this baptism of power really is? We dare not go so far as to say that the majority of praying people would not recognize the blessing if it came; but we do believe most believers are unaware of exactly what they are asking for when they plead with God for power. They are to be likened to the two Apostles who begged for the privilege of sitting, one on the right hand and the other on the left hand when Christ should sit on the throne of His glory and power; they scarcely seemed to realize that the privilege spells responsibility; that power can be entrusted only to those who are fit to receive it, and can be wielded only by those who obey its laws.

Think for a moment. How many men and women have you ever met who were obviously filled with power from on high? Only once in a while does a man arise who is baptized with power. How people crowd to hear him! How eagerly they drink in his message! They are deeply moved and uplifted. But in a month or two, or in a year or so, the flame seems to die down, and little more is heard of either the man or his message.

Very rarely, however, the Holy Spirit clothes a man with such spiritual power that he moves about for many years on fire for his Master, telling forth God's love with such attractive winsomeness that many thousands are brought into the Kingdom. Blessing abounds wherever he goes. And when his life's work is done people never cease to tell of his greatness and his power.

We often find that it is rarely the great ones on earth who are so used. Not the men of wealth and talent, not the intellectual giants; but just lowly and humble men of heart, who have had few educational advantages and no brilliant university career. Things hidden from the wise and prudent are often revealed unto babes (Matt. 11:25).

But how seldom do such men arise!

Yet two great facts must stand out clearly in every thinking mind:

1. That all power is given to Jesus Christ—not only all authority, but all *power*. And this power is *infinite*. "In him dwelleth all the fulness of the Godhead bodily." It is a significant fact that God revealed Himself to mankind as a God of power before He showed Himself a God of Love.

2. It cannot be the wish of God that any one of His children should lack power. He has no favorites. It is not according to His will that any follower of His should be a weak Christian, living a low-level life, constantly being defeated by "trivial" sins, and never witnessing for Christ, ever seeking but never getting "power from on high." This is surely an obvious fact. It is impossible to believe that God wants any of His children to be poor and feeble believers whose saintliness is only conspicuous by its absence; and who seek to be blessed while they never aspire to be a blessing.

A well-known soul-winner, meeting an undergraduate at a convention, said to him, "Have you come to give or to get?" Would not the vast majority of convention-goers reply, "To get"? Do not misunderstand me. We do indeed need "to get"—to get more and more. We shall never, through all eternity, learn all that there is to know of God. We shall still "go on to know." But how few Christian people lay themselves out "to give." And until our aim is "to give," believe me, we shall "get" but little.

The visible Church today is hampered, if not hindered,

because the majority of its members desire to be ministered unto and not to minister. Yet most of these would maintain that they are seeking "power from on high."

What, then, is the condition of affairs today?

1. We have a wonderful God of all power and might.

2. He longs to impart power to every believer.

3. God's children long for power and constantly pray for it. Yet how few are endued with power!

Is it not, then, worth while for us to spend a little time in thinking over once again this stupendous promise of the Savior: "Ye shall receive power"?

What is this "power"? Do I possess it? Is it for me? How may I get it? How does this power manifest itself? What does it fail to do? What hinders its inflow and its outflow? Can it be lost? How may it be retained? Surely there are few questions—if any—of greater importance to a Christian.

The very fact that our Lord promised "power from on high" to those disciples whose experience and work were already unique in the history of mankind shows that the need of power must be very great. If those men who had accompanied the Lord Jesus for three years and had had the amazing privilege of being taught by the Risen Master for forty days—if *those* men still needed the illumination and the power of the Holy Spirit, how much more must we require it?

Many of us work hard enough for the Master, but how fruitless are most of our lives! How inefficient and ineffective is that work! How powerless we are against Satan's guiles! What little headway we make against the forces of evil! Yet we go on our way still praying for power, but never tarrying till it comes. Not that there is any *need* for us to tarry, if only we are fit recipients of power.

We feel sure that the majority of Christian workers are disappointed because of their personal powerlessness; although the Evil One tries to persuade them that there is not need to *see results*—"One sows and another reaps," he whispers. Our Lord plainly told His disciples: "I sent you to reap."

Now the nominal Christian knows nothing of power. The casual Christian cares little about it, and it does not enter into his head even to pray for it. He is often content with the prayers he uttered as a child. Sometimes "Gentle Jesus" and "The Lord's Prayer" is all he feels he needs to ask!

Instead of yearning for power he even doubts his standing, and asks, "Am I his or am I not?" His friends, too, wonder where he is! He may be a Christian man, but he is no help to God and no hindrance to the devil. A few weeks ago a business man said to me, "Until recently I regarded the salvation of one's own soul as 'The whole duty of man.' Then I read *The Glory Christian* and it changed my entire outlook. Now I see I have a duty to others—but oh, *how I need power!* " This need of power was not even felt until he endeavored to witness for Christ.

This book is written especially for that great multitude of believers who, from a sense of duty, are working hard for their Savior, but who are conscious of a lack of power. They pray often and earnestly for the fullness of the Holy Spirit and yet nothing seems to happen in themselves or through their activities.

Sometimes they fondly imagine that if they exercise power from the human level—the power you and I exert over each other by our influence and example, our cheeriness and comradeship, that will be sufficient. *It is not so.*

There are few men—I question if there is one other—spoken of in the Scriptures in terms of such extraordinary praise as Apollos. He is spoken of as "an eloquent man and mighty in the scriptures, . . . instructed in the way of the Lord; and being fervent in the spirit, he spake and taught diligently the things of the Lord." And he spake "boldly," too (Acts 18:24—26). One ancient manuscript says that Apollos was "steeped in the Scriptures and boiling in the spirit," and that "he taught diligently and accurately." Why, one would have thought that such a man would turn the city upside down! For Paul himself had already visited Ephesus (v. 19) for a short time, and had broken the ice for him. No!

His influence was small for he knew only the baptism of John and not that of the Holy Spirit.

But knowledge of the Scriptures, and fervor and eloquence are all alike—useless without power from on high. No amount of "boiling in the spirit" can take the place of the Holy Spirit's power.

His zeal and fervor and eloquence and "accurate" book-knowledge accomplished but little. When Paul came again to Ephesus—after Apollos had left—he found only about twelve weak disciples there, and he at once detected something wrong in their life and witness. They were very useless, feeble converts. Paul evidently missed the evidence of the presence of the Holy Spirit in those men. So he asked them: "Did ye receive the Holy Spirit when ye believed?" Their reply: "Nay, we did not so much as hear whether there is a Holy Spirit" (Acts 19:2 RV).

They had been baptized only unto John's baptism (Acts 18:25). But what a change came over Apollos when Aquila and Priscilla had "expounded unto him the way of God more carefully" (v. 26 RV). Apparently he did not stop at Ephesus to put those twelve men right; and it does not seem to have occurred to Aquila and Priscilla to do so. We wonder why? Apollos went off to Achaia. We are told that "when he was come, he helped them much which had believed through grace: For he powerfully confuted the Jews, [showing] publicly by the scriptures that Jesus was the Christ" (Acts 18:27−28 RV).

Yes—when "power from on high" comes upon a believer there will be "great grace" as well as great power.

We believe that there are thousands of Christian men and women, who, like Apollos, are possessed with wonderful gifts. They are earnest and devout, full of zeal and mighty in the Scriptures, eager to serve God, and even eloquent in their appeal, and yet they see very little result from their strenuous labors.

Is it not because they are living experimentally, on the wrong side of Pentecost? The disciples in our Lord's day were converted people. They were sent forth to preach and work miracles during His life on earth, yet they were not endued with "power from on high." So we, too, may be converted folk, yet powerless. Or we may have the misfortune of having as our spiritual instructor a man as eloquent and as mighty in the Scriptures as Apollos and yet one who knows nothing of the fullness of the Spirit in his own spiritual experience. Now among God's people it is His desire that there should be "not one feeble person in all their tribes."

His plan and purpose for us is that everyone who believes on His name should be filled with power from on high.

He does not wish any follower of His, whether old or young, rich or poor, unlettered or learned, to be a weak Christian. He is able and He is willing at this very moment to strengthen "with might by his Spirit in the inner man" (Eph. 3:16) even the weakest and most faltering and most useless believer.

Let me say it again: a life without power is *not* God's plan for you and me. The Spirit-filled life is *not* a privilege reserved for the few. It is for *all*; even for *all* that are afar off.

How one longs to be able to have the joy of Aquila and Priscilla of "expounding the way of God more carefully" to some who do not know how to obtain the power God yearns to bestow.

We believe that it would be a blessed day for the Church of Christ if every believer would cease from doing inefficient, powerless service (so-called!) for the Master, and would wait till endued with power from on high. The Savior who bade *those* tarry would surely bid us tarry. We do not ask for idle tarrying. That would be worse than useless. Even feeble and fruitless and ineffective work for Christ often *drives* a man to seek for power. No—but to stop attempting the impossible task of working without power, so that every moment of available time might be spent in seeking to know and to fulfill the conditions upon which power alone is given. "Power from on high" is not given for the mere asking. There are conditions—indispensable conditions—to be fulfilled.

Oh, the pity of it all! Men are dying around us in their sins although we are earnestly striving to reach them. The world is misunderstanding Christ because we Christians are not "manifesting Christ in our mortal bodies."

Christ is expecting us to bring glory to His name and we are so often a stumbling block both to the world and to our fellow believers, simply because we lack power from on high!

God needs today not so much inspired apostles as living epistles known and read by all men. And just as God's written Word was inspired by the Holy Spirit, so must the living epistle of today be inspired by the selfsame Spirit. As Christ was overcome by the power of the Holy Spirit, so also must we (Rev. 3:21).

The greatest hindrance to the spread of the Gospel is the feeble Christian. Why *should* anyone desire to be a Christian like we are?

A Chinese gentleman was asked, "What is the greatest hindrance to the spread of Christianity in China?"

He replied, without a moment's hesitation: "The *Christian* is the greatest obstacle!"

Gandhi, who is a Bible student, was asked in his Indian prison, "Why doesn't India accept Jesus Christ?" "Because, although we reverence the Christ, we fail to see His Spirit in those who profess to believe in Him," he answered.

There we must leave the matter for the present.

God had illimitable, infinite power. He desires every one of His children to be filled with power—clothed with power from on high. We long with intense yearning for Power. The world is offended if not amazed at our weakness. And all the time God is just waiting to give us the power which is already poured forth—waiting till we are willing to fulfill the simple conditions He demands of us.

"God hath spoken once; twice have I heard this, that power belongeth unto God" (Ps. 62:11).

Then I must get God on my side—yes, and God in my heart in absolute control if I am ever to be a Power-Full Christian. For the God who said, "My glory will I not give to another," will not *give* His power to another. I can only get power by receiving the Giver of Power.

"All power is given unto me," saith Christ. But He adds, "And, lo, I am with you always."

And the Lord Jesus who ever lives to intercede for us desires "that Christ may dwell in your hearts by faith. . . . that ye might be filled with all the fulness of God" (Eph. 3:17,19). That was the prayer the Holy Spirit put into the mind and lips of Paul; and He—the Spirit—"knoweth the mind of God."

And when we are entirely and unceasingly under the control of the Holy Spirit we shall at once be filled with "power from on high."

2
Waiting for Power

Who may have this "power from on high"? And where may it be found? These questions will be answered in due course. But let us make it quite plain once and for all, that *any* believer—ignorant or learned, young or old, rich or poor— may get this power; and may get it just where he is, and may get it *now*. Whatever a man's present environment, and whatever his past record may be, he need not "tarry" a moment longer than is necessary to understand the conditions upon which "power" is given, and to fulfill those conditions, and claim the blessing.

How we praise God for that humble confession of Paul's: "Unto me, who am less than the least of all saints, is this grace given, that I should preach among the Gentiles the unsearchable riches of Christ" (Eph. 3:8).

Despite his past—blasphemer, persecutor of the saints, injurer—"power from on high" fell upon *him*.

And even though we were a thousand times more unworthy than Paul felt himself to be, we, too, may claim the blessing if we fulfill the conditions.

But let us show how beautifully the events on the day of Pentecost prove this. "Ye shall be baptized with the Holy Spirit not many days hence. But tarry ye in the City of Jerusalem until ye be endued with power from on high." So spake our Lord just before His ascension into heaven.

How amazed those men and women must have been!

Power from on high? What further "power" could they need? Surely if anyone was qualified to work and to witness for Christ, *they* were?

A year or two before that time the Lord Jesus "called his twelve disciples together and gave them power and authority over all devils and to cure diseases" (Luke 9:1). Matthew says, "He . . . gave them authority over unclean spirits, to cast them out, and to heal all manner of disease and all manner of sickness" (Matt. 10:1 ʀᴠ). The Lord Jesus said to them, "Heal the sick, raise the dead, cleanse the lepers, cast out devils: Freely [i.e., as a gift, not by merit or purchase] ye have received, freely give" (v. 8). In fact, He gave them "power over all the power of the enemy" (Luke 10:19).

The singular thing, however, is that the people or at least the Pharisees, did not recognize this power as "power from on high." They said that our Lord cast out devils by Beelzebub, the prince of the devils. And they asked Him even after He had worked many miracles, for "a sign *from heaven*"—from "above"! (Luke 11:14—16). It is clear, then, that there was a further and a greater "power" which the disciples were to expect.

Was it cleansing power? Yet Jesus Christ had already said to the twelve, "Ye are clean, but not all. For he knew who should betray him" (John 13:10—11). Still, they were to wait for *power*. Surely their curiosity must have exceeded their surprise. *What could this power be?* What would it enable them to do?

We have dwelt upon this point because we desire every reader to be filled with like curiosity. How many of us could give a clear explanation of just what the power was that the 120 received on the day of Pentecost? Have we never thought that if the Lord Jesus gave any one of us such "power" as He gave before Pentecost to the twelve, or even "the seventy," we could work marvels in His name? What an extraordinary sensation we should make! How people would flock to our ministry!

But those men of our Lord's days on earth not only did those things which they were empowered and commissioned to do. They also possessed additional "power." They had a story to tell of amazing interest and stupendous importance. They had had an experience unequaled and unique. They were our Lord's own converts. They had been His fellow-workers. That was an enormous privilege. Men who were won to God through Moody's ministry or who worked shoulder to shoulder with him, are always "telling about their salvation," or revealing by lip and life how great was Moody's inspiration. But to be one of our Lord's converts, and to company with Him! To have heard His marvelous sermons—such words as "never man spake" before. To have witnessed His wonderful miracles, and to have watched His gracious life; to have seen the Father in Him, even though they were not fully conscious of it: Why, what would not such men have to say? With what knowledge—yes, and with what power they would speak! Our Lord Himself called their attention to the unique privilege which was theirs.

He said to His disciples privately: "Blessed are the eyes which see the things ye see: For I tell you, that many prophets and kings have desired to see those things which ye see, and have not seen them; and to hear those things which ye hear, and have not heard them" (Luke 10:23–24). And this was before His death and Resurrection.

Added to all this were their own deep spiritual experiences—the doubtings, the disputings, the misunderstandings, the denial and desertion of their Lord: the apparent collapse of their faith before the horrors of the Cross, and the death of their Lord.

Then came the sight of the empty tomb and the revelation of the Risen Lord. What a reversal of feelings! What a holy joy was theirs when they realized His full and free forgiveness of all their past! How quickly those forty days of sweet communion passed as He opened up the Scriptures—wonderful days of instruction and inspiration. Then there was the Ascension into heaven and the message of the angels, "He shall come again!"

Why! if we had shared these experiences, after receiving

such miraculous power over disease and demon and death, I question if, even in our wildest dreams, we could imagine any greater "power" that could come to us. Yet there are "greater things than these."

So there rang in their ears the promise, "Ye shall receive power." "Tarry ye . . . until ye be endued with power from on high." We marvel that they could keep silence. We should have wanted to blaze abroad the wonderful things we had seen and heard. but they needed power, all the same.

So, with hearts very nearly overwhelmed with joy and praise, "These all with one accord continued steadfastly in prayer, with the women, and Mary the mother of Jesus, and with his brethren" (Acts 1:14 RV).

They waited with great expectation for *power*—a power so great that even their enemies declared later on that these Power-Full Christians had "turned the world upside down" (Acts 17:6 RV).

Now may it not be that we too have had wonderful experiences and have received a certain amount of power and have been promised a certain amount of success in our work, and yet have not received the fullness of that "power from on high"? We may even have sought vaguely for "power"—for the fullness of the Holy Spirit.

Some, I know, are waiting until they can get away for a quiet time alone with God—on the hills or in the woods, or on a lake. We would like to call attention to our Lord's clear command, "Tarry ye in the *City* of Jerusalem, until ye be endued with power from on high." We would have suggested a few quiet days in the country, perhaps in the mountains of Galilee, far from the excitement and bustle of a city at feast-time. Yet how grateful we should be for those words "in the City of Jerusalem." That was the most impossible place in which to receive spiritual blessing! It was the very last place we should ever think of. That city was thronged with people from everywhere—by "men from every nation under heaven" (Acts 2:5). For it was a feast-time. Yet that was the place chosen by our Lord in which His followers should receive this great blessing.

"The city," with its babel of voices in a score of languages: with its densely crowded streets and booths. It was that city which, a few weeks ago, had crucified their Lord, and was still hostile with the hatred of its rulers and the unbridled malice of its priests.

Jerusalem? What city could excel it in wickedness or in spurned and despised opportunities? Our Lord Himself had wept over it. "O Jerusalem, Jerusalem, which killest the prophets, and stonest them that are sent unto thee; how often would I have gathered thy children together . . . and ye would not! Behold, your house is left unto you desolate" (Luke 13:34–35).

How often! Now He comes with a blessing against their desires—forcing a blessing upon the city which had stoned His forerunners, and crucified Him, the Lord of Glory. "Taste and see how gracious the Lord is." "A few righteous" in a city can bring great blessing.

Do we not see the obvious truth? God can bless a man *anywhere*. Many who read these lines are longing for an opportunity of getting to Keswick, or Swanwick, or The Hayes, or some other well known Convention resort. If they could only get *there*, how easy it would be to experience a Pentecost! We have even heard it said by enthusiasts that the "special blessing" of Keswick can be secured nowhere else! No! It is false! "Power from on high" can come to any man in any place under any circumstances; and *will* come—*must* come—to anyone who fulfills the conditions. A few weeks ago the writer asked a professional man, "Have you ever been to Keswick?" "No," he replied, "I had my Keswick one evening in my back garden, whilst reading *How to Live the Victorious Life*."

What a comfort it is to know that God can bless me *here*, wherever I may be. Our Lord did not merely say "Tarry in Jerusalem." The disciples might then have met in some beautiful suburb, or on Olivet's slopes, or even in the quieter seclusion of Bethany. No! The command was, "Tarry ye *in the city.*" And whatever "*city*" you dwell in, dear reader, it is "there" that you may now receive "power from on high."

But there was another reason for tarrying "in the city." "Power from on high" was to be sent not just to make those 120 disciples Power-Full Christians. It was sent to bring blessings to thousands in that city. Our Lord's command was that "repentance and remission of sins should be preached in his name . . . beginning at Jerusalem" (Luke 24:47).

Had these 120 been away in the mountains of Galilee, or on the shores of the Sea of Tiberias, when the power came upon them they would have been out of touch with suffering humanity while the "fire burned within them." They might have been tempted to remain there, thinking the blessing to be linked with solitary places. Simon Peter might have cried out once more, "It is good for us to be here. Let us build a great tabernacle and enjoy this gift." Do not many people, and even congregations, act in this way? Remember that the power is only granted as we pass it on. It must flow *out* of our inmost beings (John 7:38) if it is to continue to flow *in.* The Holy Spirit is never granted merely to make us holy or happy.

Yes—the *city* was the right place. So they "tarried." Who tarried? There were at least 500 brethren who loved the Lord and had seen Him after his Resurrection (1 Cor. 15:6). But in the Upper Room were found only about 120 disciples, including women and, possibly, children, when the power came (Acts 1:15). Apparently only one in four "tarried"! Is it possible that the others did not know of the promise? It is scarcely possible that they did not know of the promise? It is scarcely possible that they did not *value* the gift of power? It may be that they were so anxious to publish abroad the tidings of the Ascension that they heeded not the command. We do not know *why* they were absent when "power from on high" came.

But this we know: God has no favorites. The promise of power is to every believer—man, woman, or child.

And we believe that the command to "tarry till ye be endued with "power from on high" is to everyone who desires to work for the Master. (Although it is unnecessary to tarry even for "not many days.") Power is never granted to idlers.

So many of us seem to go our own way "working for Christ" without the needed power. Some of us seem scarcely to know of the promise. Some Christians appear to think that God endues one here and another there with "power from on high" through the Holy Spirit coming upon them, while for some reason only known to Him, all the rest are passed by.

It is not so. The promise of the Father is for every child of God—to you and to me and to all who believe.

Listen to Peter. If ever there was a time when the Spirit of God filled and thrilled a man, burning the message into his very soul, and inspiring his lips with divine utterances, it was so with Simon Peter on the day of Pentecost. What does this Spirit-filled man say? "Repent, and be baptized every one of you in the name of Jesus Christ for the remission of sins, and ye shall receive the gift of the Holy Ghost. For the promise is unto you, . . . even as many as the Lord our God shall call" (Acts 2:38–39).

Fellow believer—*we* were once afar off, and the promise is to us. We have been "called"; praise God for that.

"But now in Christ Jesus [we] who sometimes were afar off are made nigh by the blood of Christ" (Eph. 2:13). The promise is for us; the power is for us. Have we received it? If not, *why* not?

May God the Holy Spirit guide my thoughts and my pen that *He Himself* shall make this message so plain and so clear that the dullest and most illiterate and most slow-witted of us can understand. God wants me to be a Power-Full Christian. God wants you—*every* believer—to be a Power-Full Christian.

Let us not covet the gifts and talents of others! A great

intellect is often tempted to pride and doubt. Does not the Holy Spirit seem to shine more clearly in those who have few talents?

For then it is so plainly recognized "that the excellency of the power *is* of God and not of us" (2 Cor. 3:6).

Ah! the treasure in earthen vessels seems treasure indeed! So it was on the day of Pentecost. Had those disciples been great scholars no one would have been surprised that every man heard in his own tongue (language).

The amazing thing in the minds of the rulers and the great men was not only the boldness of Peter and John but that "they were unlearned and ignorant men."

At such manifestation of power in *such men*, "they marvelled; and they took knowledge of them, that they had been with Jesus" (Acts 4:13). Only "Jesus" could account for such power. It was not the Holy Spirit they saw working, but the Lord Jesus.

Are we unlearned? Are we ignorant? Well, the promise is still the same for us all; and Christ will be glorified in us all the more.

Let us never blame our demerits or our surroundings or our position because we lack power. "Tarry . . . in the *city*. . . ."

One further word before we go on to show that neither our past failure nor the failures of others can rob us of the promise of power.

"The City of Jerusalem." What a record it had! Killing prophets—stoning God's sent-ones. Yet *even there* a mighty revival broke out because a few disciples "tarried" there and prayed there. No city is too hard, too wicked, too far gone for a revival if only the disciples there get "power from on high." But *without* that power even the most favored city will not be blessed.

3
Tarrying in the City

So they tarry in the city. Yes, in the crowded city, in the very last place which you would choose for a quiet time for seeking a blessing from on high.

But did you ever try to picture those ten days of waiting? Their Master has gone from them; they had seen Him "go into heaven"; and the angels' words are still echoing in their minds. They are bereft of their Lord, yet no one put on mourning. No tears dimmed their eyes, and no doubts or fears clouded their minds. "Great joy" filled their hearts, and they "were continually in the temple praising and blessing God."

We are told that the disciples "all continued with one accord in prayer and supplication, with the women" (Acts 1:14). Our Lord had promised them "power from on high" and no doubt this was the chief burden of their prayer; and was not their "supplication" surely for the thousands of worshipers who had come up to the feast?

What a wonderful prayer meeting that must have been! It went on for ten days with intervals for meals and sleep and perhaps for temple worship. Someone has said that those days "opened a new era in the relation of man with heaven." Yet remember that this was not "praying in the Holy Spirit"—a thing which is now possible to you and me, and is our blessed privilege.

But surely there had never been such intense and sustained united prayer as was offered up in that Upper Room. Christ had promised power "not many days hence";

so there was absolute certainty that *power would come.* Yet they continued in prayer—prayer to the Lord Jesus as well as to the Father.

Heaven and earth were full of God's glory before those waiting days, but now that the "Lord of glory" was received up into glory, Heaven was a new place to those disciples, for the Blessed Master was there interceding for them.

Before the Ascension Heaven had been an infinity of glory, but now—as William Arthur strikingly puts it—"infinity had received a center"; all the glory now converged upon the Person of the Lord Jesus Christ. And surely their prayers went up to Him now "set down on the right hand of the Majesty on High." "He shall be great," said Gabriel at our Lord's birth; and in His greatness He still intercedes for us.

Martha had once said to her Lord, "But I know that . . . whatsoever thou wilt ask of God, God will give it thee" (John 11:22). Now Christ had promised the disciples, "I *will pray the Father,* and he shall give you another Comforter, that he may abide with you for ever" (John 14:16). With what confidence and assurance those 120 disciples prayed! Christ was interceding, and they were pleading, and the Father had already promised the blessing; for our Lord speaks of the gift of the Holy Spirit as the "Promise of the Father."

Carry your thoughts back, then, to that Upper Room. As they pray our Savior's words keep ringing in their minds, "tarry ye . . . till ye be endued with power from on high." "Ye shall receive power when the Holy Ghost is come upon you. John indeed baptized with water, but ye shall be baptized with the Holy Spirit not many days hence."

Surely some of them remembered the prediction of John the Baptist: "He shall baptize you with the Holy Ghost and fire" (Luke 3:16). What could it all mean? The story of Moses and the burning bush; the wonders of the Shekinah glory in the Holy of Holies of the tabernacle of old; the prophecies of Ezekiel and Isaiah, and the live coal off the altar that touched his lips all began to acquire a fresh meaning and importance. But those disciples evidently spent their time chiefly in prayer. Ah! There was *joy* in that prayer meeting. They were all filled with *certain hope.*

So they prayed and prayed. So they waited and waited. "Not many days hence." Did they half hope that the power would fall that very night? The singular thing is that no one seemed to have longed to have the dear Master back again. They believed His word: "It is expedient for you that I go away, for if I go not away the Comforter will not come unto you." Yet they must have wondered *how* the Comforter could ever be to them what Christ had been. But He said they would really be better off with the Holy Spirit than with Himself. This must have seemed incredible—but it was true, and is equally true for us as well. There *is* a sense in which we may sing:

> I think when I read that sweet story of old,
> When Jesus was here among men,
> How He call'd little children as lambs to His fold!
> I should like to have been with Him then!

But, believe me, *we may know Jesus Christ* far better than those who lived with Him in Galilee and Judaea.

With what intense longings they must have prayed for this mysterious and indispensable "power from on high," as they looked away to Christ Jesus seated at the right hand of God—"glorified, adored and owned."

Did they pray all through that Thursday night? Surely excessive joy and ardent longing would forbid sleep? Friday dawned—the day of the week on which the Lord was crucified; will the power fall today? The first day of the week comes around. Surely the baptism of fire will be theirs today: the day on which the Lord Jesus rose from the dead?

How the words must have sprung to their lips time after time! Yet still they waited. It never occurred to Thomas to absent himself in unbelief; nor to Simon Peter to cry, "I go a-fishing." But no doubt they began to marvel at the delay. They were longing to tell their glad tidings—to "go into all the world and preach the Gospel," as Jesus had once commanded them. How men needed that Gospel! Multitudes were dying in their sins, not knowing that Christ had died for them; and yet the disciples were bidden to hold their peace—to tarry till *power* came from on high!

Why this delay? Was it not to deepen their sense of utter dependence upon the Holy Spirit? Simon Peter, however, began to think that something must be done. So he set to work choosing an apostle. I question if this was God's will. He said, "Tarry." And later on He Himself called Saul of Tarsus to the apostolic band. But Christ Jesus did not allow this act of Peter to hinder the bestowal of "power."

"Not many days hence." Nine days go by, and still the power does not fall. Whose fault is it?

They want power. They have prayed earnestly and in faith. They have praised with hearts overflowing with joy, and yet the blessing does not come! Now if we had been there should we not have been tempted to put the blame on someone?

Unless Satan missed a great opportunity, those waiting men and women must have been sorely tempted to suggest that the hindrance to blessing lay in someone's heart. There were several disciples there whom the Church today would have hesitated to entrust with power.

How easy it would have been to criticize others! As they looked around they might have thought—and even *said*— "No wonder the power does not come with Thomas among us! We know his doubting disposition. Why, he even refused to accept our united testimony that the Lord was risen indeed! No doubt there is still unbelief lurking secretly in his heart." Want of faith is quite enough to prevent God from doing any "mighty work."

Then what about Simon Peter? Is he quite free from blame? It is not so long ago that he denied his Lord with oaths and curses! He can scarcely be trusted with power to witness—with those lips—for the Master yet! Surely he must have a year or two of probation before he is quite reliable!

Think of the sons of Zebedee: why, they actually sought and *asked for* the two chief places in Christ's kingdom! It is impossible for God to grant power to self-seekers! They would use it for their own glorification. And we remember how they once wished to call down fire from heaven to burn up those who opposed their way (Luke 9:54). Such hotheads cannot be trusted with "power from on high."

And could we have blamed the women if they had begun to suspect that the *disciples* were the hindrance to the bestowal of blessing? Did they not all forsake Him and flee in the hour of His direst need? The men, too, might have felt that the women were to blame. Look at Mary Magdalene— why, she was once possessed with seven devils (Luke 8:2). How can we expect the Holy Spirit to dwell in all His fullness in a heart so lately tenanted by evil spirits? Ah, how easy it would have been to blame others!

In these "enlightened days" it is possible that the women might even be requested to withdraw from the assembly (It is a dreadful suggestion!). They would be told that "witnessing" was the work of men, and not of women. The writer has known men of God threatening to have nothing more to do with a united mission if a woman—whom they recognized as fully sanctified—was allowed to preach in a church, even to women only. God help us!

Yet the Lord Jesus made a woman the first messenger of the news of His Resurrection. Those who forbid the ministry of women need to come in contact with some godly and devout Priscilla who could "expound unto [them] the way of God more perfectly" (Acts 18:26).

Those saintly women in that Upper Room were a help— not a hindrance. And they, too, were soon all filled with the Holy Spirit.

That great and incomparable blessing of "power from on high" fell upon every one of those 120 disciples, in spite of all their past failings and their present unworthiness. Mary Magdalene was blessed equally with Mary the Mother of our Lord!

Forgive us for emphasizing this point. We are all so prone to murmur about others, and to blame their faults and shortcomings for *our own lack* of power.

Let us, however, make no mistake in our views on sin. Our blessed Lord never excused sin and never condoned sin. Sin *is always a curse*. It is never a blessing in disguise and never brings an added blessing to one who repents. There is a sense in which we *may*—

rise on stepping stones of our dead selves to higher things.

But we never get higher *because we have* sinned. Sin is never a "fall upwards."

Our Lord pointed out that in one way we may be "loved most" because we are the "most forgiven" (Luke 7:42–43). But is is utterly wrong to imagine that among forgiven sinners the one whose sins were greatest has an advantage over those whose sins were less.

There is a tendency to think that it is easier for God to make a holy and deeply spiritual saint out of an utterly vile and sinful savage, who has been converted, than out of a good-living moral man who turns to Him. But it is not so.

It is never an advantage to have sinned. But if our repentance is "true and deep," *no blessing is withheld from us because of past sins*. John, who once asked that fire from heaven might fall on the Samaritans, was even allowed to be the human instrument of calling down the fire of the Holy Spirit upon them! (Acts 8:14).

Great sinners do indeed sometimes become great saints— as in the case of the once-lascivious St. Augustine. As a rule, however, "the lingering taint of bygone years" is detrimental to great holiness—*although it need not be.*

Now we want "power from on high": we *all* want it. We long for it ardently. We pray for it fervently, and we wonder why it does not come upon us, upon our Church, upon our cause, upon our town.

Are we *looking around* for the hindrance, instead of looking within? How often the pastor blames a worldly flock! How often the flock blames an unspiritual pastor! The individual is prone to attribute his own lack of power to the deadness and coldness of the other members of his church. If only *they* were sincere; if only *they* really sought the fullness of the Holy Spirit; how different—how *easy* it would be!

Now we have already seen that environment cannot hinder God from blessing us. Pentecost came to those seeking souls, not in the seclusion of some quiet and peaceful resort, but in the most impossible of places—a hostile and crowded city at the time of a "religious" festival.

And in this chapter we are laying stress upon the fact that each man for himself may lay claim to "power from on high" whatever may be the lack of spiritual attainments among his friends. For the Holy Spirit has been poured forth and already dwells in the heart of every believer.

No man but yourself can rob you of the fullness of blessing. No man is deprived of any spiritual gift because of the faults and failing of others. The "unworthiness of the minister" need not deprive you of power. And the unworthiness of the flock cannot of itself keep back the pastor from obtaining God's gifts.

Fenton Hall, that wonderfully consecrated and devoted missionary to Amazonia, wrote in his diary: "Probably there is only one man on board this ship who can spoil that which God would do, and *that man is I.*"

And only one man can keep *you* back from becoming a Power-Full Christian *and that man is you yourself.* Environment cannot prevent: you can be filled in the city as well as on the mountain-top. Half-hearted and cold fellow Christians need not hinder. *You,* and you alone, can prevent God from blessing *you.* St. Augustine used to pray, "O God, save me from my greatest enemy—myself!" And we all might well pray the same.

Remember that Aaron's rod budded and blossomed and bore fruit even when tied up with a bundle of dry sticks! (Num. 17:6−8).

What a marvelous revelation of God's patience and love we have in Pentecost! What a lesson of deepest comfort sinful men see there! Evidently no one is unfitted to receive spiritual blessing because of the sins of the past.

Those disciples, waiting in the Upper Room for power,

would remember with overwhelming joy that their friends could charge them with, but even the secret faults known only to God and to themselves.

He knew all about them, and yet, in spite of all this the blessed Master had promised them that they should be baptized with "power from on high"—not many days hence. Unworthy as they were, the promise had passed His lips and would most surely be fulfilled.

We think that they must have taken comfort even from the recollection of the Master's rebukes in the past!

He who had said to James and John, "Ye know not what manner of spirit ye are of" (Luke 9:55); He who had said to Simon Peter, "Get thee behind me, Satan!"—and to His mother, "Woman, what have I to do with thee?" He who had said to Thomas, "Be not faithless, but believing"—He it was who promised power to these selfsame men, with all their faults.

But perhaps some who read these words are saying, "Yes, that is all true. Yet even so, I am far more unworthy than the least of His disciples. I cannot for a moment rank myself with even the most faulty of those 120 in the Upper Room!" We would ask such timorous and hesitating folk to read again the words of John the Baptist—the man "filled with the Holy Ghost, even from his mother's womb" (Luke 1:15).

It was to the Pharisees and Sadducees of all people—the most bitter and constant of our Lord's opponents—to whom the Baptist first said, "He shall baptize you with the Holy Ghost, and with fire" (Matt. 3:11). And this wonderful declaration of them: "O generation of vipers" (v. 7)!

O my brothers, if God could change the hearts of the Pharisees—those moral, zealous, self-denying, but self—righteous men, destitute of all sense of sin and need; and of those Sadducees who not only denied that there was any resurrection, but disbelieved in the very existence of angels and other spirits, and fill *such* men with the Holy Spirit, there is hope for every one of us.

Eternity itself will not be long enough for us to fathom all the boundless grace and goodness of our God!

He is not only able, but *willing* to lift a man from the lowest depth of iniquity to the greatest height of holiness.

There died in America two summers ago, a man whose record was so despicable that he was probably one of the greatest criminals in the United States. After years of vice and crime, during which time he had been expelled from the city of his birth and forbidden ever to return; twice turned out of the army and once out of the navy, as too vile a man to be in the ranks, a boon companion laughingly taunted him with being afraid to attend a mission service! He went to scoff and to mock. God met him there, convicted him of sin, and drew him to the Cross of Christ for pardon and deliverance. He quickly became one of the most saintly men in America.

For years he—the Rev. William Jacoby—was assistant to Dr. Torrey in Chicago. Dr. Torrey, who had traveled all over the world and had come in contact with the leading Christian men of all continents, said that, without exception, Jacoby was the most holy and most loved man he had ever met!

Think of it! Let the marvel of it take hold of you. May it inspire us all to fulfill the conditions and to claim power from on high, if we have not already done so.

The writer told the story of this wonderful man—wonderful only because of the grace of God—in a church one morning. The vicar immediately stood up and said, "A few years back Mr. Jacoby was my guest in this very parish for three weeks, and while he lived in my vicarage my home was like heaven on earth."

Now God can do the same for you and me. Is it not an extraordinary thing that *any* Christian man or woman should remain powerless—useless?

Is it not an extraordinary thing that we should—*any of us*—go stumbling on, with lives so feeble and fruitless? Each of us knows a little of his own unworthiness; but the Lord Jesus knows it all.

Thank God, His grace is sufficient for us.

The words of Peter still ring in our ears, "The promise is to *you,* and to your *children, and to all that are afar off*" (Acts 2:39).

Are we hesitating and lamenting because we *are* so "far off"? Why, that is an added proof that the promise is *for us!* We are quite certain it is for all—for all who are willing to fulfill the conditions.

We need have no fear. Every grievous failure of the past is known to Him. All the dark sins of our unregenerated days are known to Him. Yes—and what is more deplorable, all our failures since our conversion are naked and open in His sight. But, beloved, we have been "called." We have heard the call and answered it, and the promise is to us.

If we have not received "power from on high" it cannot be because we have become unfitted to receive it, but only because we are not willing to allow the Lord Jesus to make us meet for the Master's use.

No past sin, whether of doubt, or denial, or cursing, or selfseeking need prevent us from receiving the blessing.

There is not one of us too far off, too low down, too sin-stained to enter the ranks of the Power-Full Christians, if only we will let the Master deal with us as He sees fit. And is it not worth while?

If, with all our heart, we truly seek this blessing we shall most surely find it. And it may be found today—at once—*now!*

4
What is
the Power?

What is "power from on high"? What is it that makes a weak Christian a Power-Full Christian?

When those 120 disciples assembled in that Upper Room with the vision of the Ascension in their minds, and the Master's promise still ringing in their ears, what did they expect to receive? What did they actually receive? "Ye shall receive power, after the Holy Ghost is come upon you" (Acts 1:8).

Now every believer has the Holy Spirit dwelling within him. For "if any man have not the Spirit of Christ, he is none of his" (Rom. 8:9). But not every believer has power. What was it, then, that the 120 believers "received" on the day of Pentecost?

The Holy Spirit is the Third Person of the Godhead. He is God. We cannot have more or less of God. So, then, "power" must come not from our getting more of the Holy Spirit, but by allowing the Holy Spirit *to have more of* us. To be "*filled* with the Holy Spirit" is to allow the Holy Spirit to have all there is of us, so that we become unhindered partakers "of the power of an endless life" (Heb. 7:16). To "consecrate" means to "fill your hand" (see Exod. 32:29 RV marg.). When we consecrate ourselves to God we "fill our hand," as it were, *with* God! Nothing of self but "Jesus only." When our "hands" are filled with God; we are filled with the Holy Spirit and *power.*

"There are a great many people who think that what they need is a second blessing," says Dr. Stuart Holden, "whereas what they really need is to understand the first blessing, and to know and to appropriate what is really theirs in Christ Jesus."

"My grace is sufficient for you." said our Lord to Paul. "The Lord Jesus is sufficient, yet *insufficient* when not wholly and solely embraced." So said the saintly Tersteegen.

The Power-Full Christian, then, is not one who has more of the Holy Spirit than others, but one who allows the Holy Spirit to have complete control over the *will*, the affections, the desires. The Holy Spirit is allowed to dwell in the hearts of many believers, more as a privileged prisoner than as Sovereign Lord and King!

The Holy Spirit comes not as a "power" for me to use, but as a Power who desires to use *Me*. We are praying, waiting, longing for God to give us something more. But He is waiting till we *give Him* all we have and all we are, for *His use*.

"*All power* is given unto me," said Christ. (The word used there means "authority", but He has "might," too. Christ, then, has the power and He desires to manifest that power *in me and through me*.

The final choice rests with me—with *my will*—whether I shall limit the power of the Holy One (Ps. 78:41), or whether I allow the "Word of the Lord" to have "free course and be glorified" (2 Thess. 3:1). Is it not, then, a most important thing that we should get to know what this "power from on high" really is? And how it manifests itself?

There are countless thousands of Christian people who are thoroughly disappointed with themselves and with their spiritual condition. They pray and pray for the baptism of the Holy Spirit. Sometimes they go on praying for thirty, forty, or fifty years and yet, they confess, they never get the blessing. Meanwhile they are often full of good works, but not "fruitful in every good work," because they are not "increasing in the knowledge of God" (Col. 1:10).

What are they looking for?—waiting for? Let us go back in mind to that Upper Room to the very early hour which found the disciples assembled for prayer; for by nine o'clock in the morning the *Power* had come, and they were in the streets of Jerusalem making the "power" felt by all with whom they came into contact.

There they were, with one accord—no discord in their hearts, no doubts in their mind—all agreed in waiting for, pleading for, and *expecting*, the power.

It came suddenly. "Suddenly there came from heaven a sound as of the rushing of a mighty wind, and it filled all the house where they were sitting. And there appeared unto them tongues parting asunder, like as of fire; and it sat upon each of them. And they were all filled with the Holy Spirit, and began to speak with other tongues, as the Spirit gave them utterance" (Acts 2:2–4 RV). The Power had come.

Was it the Lord Jesus, now in heaven, breathing upon them once again, as He had done before in that Upper Room, when He said, "Receive ye the Holy Ghost"? (John 20:22). For this "wind" was no ordinary wind. It came neither from the east not west, neither from north nor south; it came from heaven—from "on high." "Thou hearest the sound thereof" (John 3:8). The multitude outside seems to have heard the sound, too (v. 6). Perhaps the house itself was shaken. (see Acts 4:31).

They could have no possible doubt that "the power" had come. Peter explained to the multitude that "Jesus . . . therefore being by the right hand of God exalted, and having received of the Father the promise of the Holy Spirit, he hath shed forth this, which ye now see and hear" (Acts 2:32–33).

What did they see? What did they hear? And just what was the power? An hour before, those disciples were not fit to witness for Christ. Now they are fit, and through their witnessing a mighty revival broke out in that hostile city! What a difference was there in those 120 disciples before and after that gift of power! There was a difference which could not be summed up in "boldness."

The Apostles, and doubtless the seventy, had often

preached, and preached boldly, before that day, but the Holy Spirit had not considered it worth while to record even *one* of their sermons, nor even the outline of one. But now that they are filled with the Holy Spirit, He gives us Simon Peter's sermon at length! They were converted men and women before Pentecost. They were clear, because of the word which Christ had spoken unto them (John 15:3), before Pentecost. But now they are different men; power-full men. We, too, may be disciples—converted men—yet *unfit for service* although we are working so hard for the Master. No man is fit to serve God unless filled with "power from on high."

If we claim this indispensable gift, what are we to expect: the rushing wind, the shaken house, the tongues of fire, and the other tongues of speech? Are these always the accompaniments of the gift of power? *Are these indeed the "power"?*

Now let us first of all bear in mind that the sound of the rushing wind, the fiery tongues, the gift of speaking in "other tongues," and the shaken house were only accompaniments of the power. They were signs and manifestations to call attention to the power, and not the power itself. God could have dispensed with any or all of them, as He often and usually does today. Such signs may be given in these days, or they may not. Moreover, the "gift" of speaking in "other tongues" is no proof whatever that the speaker is filled with the Holy Spirit. And the fact that a consecrated man has never spoken in an unknown tongue does not prove that he is not filled with God's Holy Spirit. (Many who read these lines may wonder what we are talking about; they are in total ignorance of the existence of people who today speak in other tongues. Nevertheless, this is a question which is causing much heart searching and much controversy. We cannot enter into controversy, but we must give a warning concerning what may be a "grave danger.")

May we, therefore, briefly answer the question: Do these signs always accompany the gift of the Holy Spirit's power? We would at once and emphatically answer, No! There was:

1. *The Rushing Wind.* Sometimes it happens that when one is baptized with power from on high he seems to feel the very breath of God upon him. It was so with Charles G. Finney. Speaking of this enduement with "power," he says, "The Holy Spirit descended upon me in a manner that seemed to go through me, body and soul. I could feel the impression like a wave of electricity going through and through me. Indeed, it seemed to come in a wave of liquid love. . . . It seemed like the breath of God. I can recollect distinctly that it seemed to fan me like immense wings." Yet many Christian people who are, without doubt, endued with power from on high have never experienced anything like that. God seems to deal with no two men alike. The Holy Spirit gives "to each one severally even as he will" (1 Cor. 12:11 RV).

2. *Tongues of Fire.* Neither is the gift of power always coupled with tongues of fire "sitting" upon the head.

Few people, if any, claim that fire-tongues are an indispensable sign. That phenomenon probably does not occur, or occurs very rarely today. The writer was told some twenty years ago that tongues of fire were seen upon the heads of a prayer group in India, so that onlookers were alarmed and hastened to get water to quench the "fire." But even if such a thing does happen today, as indeed it *may,* it must be of uncommonly rare occurrence. It is certainly not the experience of every spirit-filled believer.

It would seem that at Pentecost the fiery tongues and the rushing wind were sent to assure the 120 disciples that the gift of power had indeed come. Just as at a later date, when some of the disciples were praying for boldness "the place was shaken wherein they were gathered together" (Acts 4:31 RV).

3. *Speaking in Other Tongues.* While it is granted that the rushing wind, the shaken house and fiery tongues are not a necessary accompaniment of the gift of power, we are told by some very devoted, but mistaken, people that you cannot receive the fullness of the Holy Spirit unless you

speak in other tongues! Again and again anxious inquirers write me: "Can I be baptized with power from on high, if I do not speak in other tongues?" Most assuredly you can. Neither do you need to take up serpents or drink deadly poisons to prove that you "believe" (Mark 16:17−19). The vast majority of believers who have been "baptized with the Holy Spirit and with the power" have never received the "gift" of tongues, and probably never will do so, nor is there any need for them to do so. Paul himself answered this question when he wrote, "Are all apostles? Are all prophets? . . . Do all speak with tongues?" (1 Cor. 12:29−30). No, they do not. Even *all* Spirit-filled believers do not so speak. But Satan is endeavoring to bring ridicule, derision, and discredit upon the cause of Christ; and doubt and division to His followers.

We have already pointed out that even the working of miracles is no proof whatever of the possession of "power from on high." Quite early in His ministry our Lord said that on the great Judgment Day many will say, "Lord, Lord, did we not prophesy in thy name, and by thy name cast out demons, and by thy name do many mighty works?" ("powers," the very same Greek word as "power" from on high) "And then," says Christ, "will I profess unto them, I never knew you. Depart from me *ye that work iniquity"!* (Matt. 7:22−23).

Those men there described are perfectly sincere. They are so confident that they are all right that they remind the Great Judge of their good deeds, and maintain that they were done in His name! "Workers of iniquity" our Lord calls them. Their "marvels" and those "powers" were the work not of the Holy Spirit but of Satan himself!

So, then, gifts resembling those of the Holy Spirit may appear even in unworthy lives. Moreover, miracles often fail to convince the world of sin, which conviction is the special work of the Holy Spirit (John 16:8−9). The only cities which our Lord upbraided for their unbelief were those in which most of His mighty works (Greek—"Powers") were done! (Matt. 11:20).

We need not yearn for miraculous gifts. We need not covet the rod of Moses, the cloak of Elijah, the harp of David, the wisdom of Solomon, or the tongues of Pentecost. John the Baptist did no miracle, although filled with the Holy Spirit even from his mother's womb. Other men who did work miracles and professed to do them in Christ's name, were found to be workers of iniquity (Matt. 7:23). They knew nothing of the Holy Spirit's power. If Satan can enable men to do "Many mighty works" in the name (apparently) of Christ, he can also, as easily, cause men to speak in any tongue. So that, even if a man does speak in "other tongues," it is no proof whatever that he is filled with "power from on high."

We do not wish to be misunderstood. We are far from suggesting that the "gift" of tongues is today *only* from the evil one. We are only protesting against those who put undue emphasis on speaking in tongues. Miracles are performed today in the name and also in the power of Jesus Christ, as all of us know who have taken the trouble to investigate the matter.

We believe that God *does* sometimes still endow people with the gift of speaking in other tongues. Yet at the same time we would earnestly warn believers against any desire to seek such a "gift," which is frequently counterfeited by Satan. It seems incomprehensible that God should, in these days, wish anyone to speak in some unintelligible language to please Himself. Bible students will have noticed that the Scriptures never speak of "unknown" tongues. Where the word "unknown" occurs in the Authorized Version it is always in italics to show that it is not the original Greek. The Revised Version rightly omits the word "unknown" (see 1 Cor 14:2, 13, 14, 19, and 27).

The Holy Spirit never speaks a lifeless word. Every word of His is full of power.

On the day of Pentecost the gift of tongues was necessary to convince that cosmopolitan multitude of the reality of the outpouring of the Holy Spirit, and to enable those people "from every nation under heaven," to understand the message, for printing was not yet known.

In the house of Cornelius a repetition of the miracle was granted. "For they heard them speak with tongues and magnify God" (Acts 10:46). This was necessary in order to show that "on the Gentiles also was poured out the gift of the Holy Ghost" (v. 45), "Even as on us (Jews) at the beginning" (Acts 11:15). *Their* Pentecost was as impressive and as full as that of the Jews. Peter himself needed this demonstration of power to convince him of the fact; and also to exonerate him form the unfair censure which other "apostles and brethren" subjected him to (Acts 11:2–18). For had those Gentiles not spoken with tongues, what proof could Peter have brought forward to his Jerusalem colleagues of the reality of the outpouring? "But, as it was, he was able to stand up before the council and ask, 'Who was I, that I could withstand God?' "

When the Holy Spirit fell upon the Samaritans, however, we hear nothing of the gift of tongues (Acts 8:17).

Remember that as early as the days of Paul a warning had to be given concerning this much-debated gift of tongues (1 Cor. 14). And that warning is needed even more today. He says, "In the Church I had rather speak five words with my understanding . . . than ten thousand words in a tongue" (v. 19 RV).

Someone wrote from Sweden that "a so-called Pentecostal movement is spreading itself over this country. . . . The gift of tongues seems to be the only object of attainment"! Satan would be delighted if he could induce Christians to spend all their time seeking such a "gift." Dr. C. I. Scofield rightly— we think—sums up Paul's teaching when he says, "Tongues and the sign-gifts are to cease, and meantime must be used with restraint and only if an interpreter is present" (1 Cor. 12: 1–19, 27–28).

The "prince of the power of the air" is still "the spirit that worketh in the children of disobedience" (Eph. 2:2). But he especially delights to get hold of devout and earnest believers to lead them astray. For it is not the avowed enemies of Christ Jesus who lay such emphasis on "tongues," but often sincere and delightful followers of our Lord and Savior.

We may be quite sure of this:

1. The Holy Spirit *always speaks to be understood.*

At Pentecost every man heard in his own tongue wherein he was born. There was a *need* for tongues then.

2. "Tongues are for a sign, not to them that believe but to them that believe not" (1 Cor. 14:22). Not a proof that one has received "power from on high," but a "marvel" to arrest the careless and godless.

3. Whenever you find the gift of tongues in people who are *proud* of the fact, and consider themselves superior Christians because of it, *that "gift" is not* from the Holy Spirit.

The more "power of the Holy Spirit" possessed by a believer, the greater will be his humility, his gentleness, and his love for others. You will never find a Spirit-filled Christian demanding proofs of holiness from another! He would rather put others before himself. No "gift" is good unless used in a spirit of love (1 Cor. 13). If the "gift" of tongues leads a man "to trust in himself that he is righteous" and makes him "despise others" you may be sure that the "gift" is not from God (Luke 18:9).

4. To *every* believer is given a spiritual enablement for service. The *lowest* of these gifts is "diversities of tongues" (1 Cor. 12:28). In the distribution of these gifts, the Holy Spirit acts according to his own sovereign will (v. 11). There is no room whatsoever for self-choosing or for judging others who do not possess the particular gift which is bestowed upon us. No gift is a *proof* of God's favor, nor does the absence of any particular gift show that we fall short of the fullness of blessing. "The manifestation of the Spirit is given to *every* man to profit withall" (v. 7).

5. Any gift of tongues which does not lead to the edification of saints and the conversion of sinners, but ends in spiritual pride and self-adulation, is *not* of the Holy Spirit.

Do not the Scriptures warn us of the danger of "seducing spirits"? "The Spirit saith expressly that in latter times some shall fall away from the faith, giving heed to seducing spirits and doctrines of devils" (1 Tim. 4:1). Whether the gift of tongues is, in any special instance, from God or from evil spirits can easily be determined.

"Beloved," says John, "believe not every spirit, but prove the spirits, whether they are of God: because many false prophets have gone out into the world. Hereby know ye the Spirit of God: every spirit which confesseth that Jesus Christ is come in the flesh is of God, and every spirit which confesseth not Jesus is not of God. . . ." (1 John 4:1–3 RV).

The danger of being ruled by an evil spirit is a real one. In the very chapter in which Paul deals with the gift of tongues he himself gives us a "test" whereby we may prove the spirits. "I give you to understand that no man speaking by the Spirit of God calleth Jesus accursed; and that no man say that Jesus is the Lord, but by the Holy Spirit" (1 Cor. 12:3).

Let us make it quite plain once more that we are not criticizing or condemning those earnest people who lay such stress upon the "gift of tongues." All we desire to do, is to prove that this "gift" is *not* a necessary accompaniment and sign of the reception of "power from on high"; nor does the ability to speak in tongues necessarily prove that the speaker is inspired by God's Holy Spirit.

"Power from on high" is not limited to miracle working, to tongues of fire, to tongues of speech, or to the "shaken place." These were all the transitory accompaniments of power; and the permanent manifestation are more important than the transitory.

The Power-Full Christ receives an abiding power which makes itself felt in life even more than in lip. Eloquence, persuasiveness, logic, learning, lucidity, "tongues" are all useless without power from on high. But *with it* all these may be dispensed with, if need be. Paul said, "My speech and my preaching was not with enticing words of man's wisdom, but in demonstration of the Spirit and of power" (1 Cor. 2:4).

The most remarkable thing about the "gift of tongues" today is that it is never given where it would seem to be of most value. There are always hundreds of missionaries overseas spending long years endeavoring to learn some strange language. It is not unusual for devoted men and women to be obliged to return home because they cannot master the language of the people among whom they long to work. A gift of tongues to these earnest servants of God would be of incalculable value. Yet, although the Holy Spirit undoubtedly aids them in their studies, we never hear of a single instance of a missionary suddenly receiving a super-natural knowledge of a foreign language—not even in the case of those who have experienced the "gift of tongues." (Some have indeed gone abroad because in a moment of ecstasy they spoke in the language of some heathen race, but have discovered to their sorrow that they are not permanently endowed with that power.) This strange fact must at least cause us to exercise very grave caution with regard to the "gift of tongues."

Few men have been more mightily endued with power or more wonderfully used of God than David Brainerd. He spent hours in prayer for the American Indians, and while not knowing their language he spoke to them in English—a tongue unfamiliar to them—and scores of these untutored people fell upon their faces and yielded themselves to God! The Holy Spirit can dispense with the "gift of tongues" when a man is filled with "power from on high."

God can do more by a *look* from a Spirit-filled man than by the words of an unsanctified Christian, whatever "tongue" he may speak.

The highest reach of genius falls far short of the lowest measure of inspiration.

What, then, signalizes "power from on high"? What *is* power? Our Lord has told us very clearly what the Holy

Spirit does in us and for us, and that therefore must be "power."

He told us that:

1. "He, when he is come, will convict the *world* in respect of sin, and of righteousness, and of judgment" (John 16:8 RV).

2. "He shall guide you into all the truth" (v. 13). "He shall declare unto you the things that are to come" (v. 13) "He shall glorify me" (v. 14). "He shall take of mine and shall declare it unto you" (v. 14). "He shall teach you all things and bring to your remembrance all that I said unto you" (John 14:26 RV).

The work, then, of the Holy Spirit is to reveal Christ to us in a new way; to bring us to a fuller understanding of the mind and the love of Christ Jesus, and to glorify Him in us and through us. The Holy Spirit is like a telescope bringing Christ and the things of Christ nearer. He is like a microscope, making the invisible things of Christ visible and surpassingly wonderful and beautiful. But neither telescope nor microscope is of much use unless focused to our eye. Every believer has the Spirit of Christ dwelling in him, but the Holy Spirit brings everything of Christ into clear spiritual focus when He has complete control and full sway over us. And He also sheds a light upon the Lord Jesus and His "truth" never seen before.

The understanding is enlightened in a marvelous way. All things become new.

After George Müller had surrendered himself fully to the Lord Jesus and had claimed the baptism of the Holy Spirit, he said, "I shut myself into my room to give myself to prayer and meditation over the Scriptures; and I learned more in a few hours than I had done during a period of several months previously."

Every believer is in Christ as the branch is in the vine. But with so many of us there are hindrances allowed to remain which prevent the flow of the sap through us; hindrances to the inflow of divine life, and to the outflow of that life in blessing to others. Allow those hindrances to go, and at once the Holy Spirit makes us *know* the Lord Jesus as never before: "Whom to know is life eternal."

The Lord Jesus is never seen until the Holy Spirit opens the eyes. He is never seen in all His beauty and glory, and felt in all His power until the Holy Spirit enlightens and illuminates the understanding, and so "glorifies Christ."

"Power from on high" is power to receive more abundantly the life of Christ in order that we may reveal that life to others. But such knowledge, such revelation of the Lord Jesus, given by the Holy Spirit, is only possible to those who obey Him. It is those who do Christ's will, *and only those,* who know of the doctrine. Only the pure in heart can see God, and *know* Him. Christ gives us power just in the proportion of the entireness of our surrender to Him.

The full consecration by which we put ourselves—out aims, our work, our plans, our *lives*—utterly into the hand of God is the only pathway to power.

"Power from on high" is that intense revelation and *realization* of Jesus Christ in the heart of a man which makes his religion and his witness a reality.

What does this mean? It simply means that people see the life of Christ in us. They recognize, and we know, that Christ dwells in our hearts through faith and that we are filled "unto all the fullness of God." They see that we are not seeking our own interests, pleasure, ease, or reputation. Our lives proclaim the message: "I have been crucified with Christ; yet I live; and yet no longer I, but Christ liveth in me" (Gal. 2:20 RV).

The Power-Full Christian is one who holds up the picture of Christ—no, the Christ Himself—that not even his own finger-tips are seen. He is one who seeks *only the glory of Jesus Christ his Lord.*

So he will be able to say in all humility and with deep joy and gratitude, "It pleased God . . . to reveal his Son in me" (Gal. 1:15–16). He will be able to say with Paul, "They glorified God in me"(v. 24).

Thus, we find Paul praying for his converts "that the name of our Lord Jesus may be glorified in you, and ye in him" (2 Thess. 1:12).

That is it. "That the life also of Jesus may be manifested in our body . . . in our mortal flesh" (2 Cor. 4:10—11 RV).

Blessed be the Lord Jesus who has given such power unto men! When we remember all that Christ Jesus is to us and *can* be to us; and when we remember all that He can be *through our lives and ministry* to a sin-burdened, distracted world, it is a marvel that any believer should hold back and refuse or hesitate to yield himself wholly to God.

It is not that we are ignorant of His riches in glory in Christ Jesus. It is not that we doubt His *willingness* to make all grace abound unto us. It is not that we doubt His *power.* Yet somehow, even earnest and devoted men of God hesitate to take this step of full surrender, which leads to power. Now once again we have been brought face to face with Christ's claims and Christ's promises. Today—*now* — shall we not commit our way, and ourselves, unto the Lord to be guided, controlled, empowered and abundantly blessed and used by Him?

To be wholly yielded is to be fully wielded; and to be fully wielded by His pierced hands is to be indeed a Power-Full Christian.

"I beseech you, therefore, brethren, by the mercies of God, to present your bodies a living sacrifice, holy, acceptable (well-pleasing) to God, which is your reasonable service. And be not fashioned according to this world: but be ye transformed by the renewing of your mind, that ye may prove what is the good and acceptable and perfect will of God" (Rom. 12:1—2 RV).

5
But I Am
a Success

Of all the Evangelists whom it has been my privilege to meet, very few have impressed me so much as the late Dr. Wilbur Chapman. His winsome way of pleading with sinners, the love that shone in his eyes, the gracious words that proceeded from his lips will never be forgotten by those who had the joy of hearing him.

But he was not always like that. He never tired of telling how a crisis came into his life in the midst of a "most successful" ministry in a wealthy church.

At what seemed to be the height of his fame Mr. Moody paid him a visit. He came to listen, not to lead.

What congregations! What preaching! What liberality! What enthusiasm! No wonder that Wilbur Chapman felt justly proud of it all. But Mr. Moody appeared to be very quiet, and obviously quite unimpressed.

At the close of what seemed to be a most wonderful day, that dear saint of God laid his hand very tenderly on Wilbur Chapman's shoulder and said, "Do you know you are a failure here? You are making a great mistake in your ministry. What you are doing does not count for much. Your preaching is not winning souls. I say it to you in all brotherly kindness." Kindness? But where did truth come in? What church could rival, or even compare with his? Was it not acclaimed by everybody as a marvelous success?

The rebuke wounded him deeply, and for days and weeks he smarted under it. Yet in his heart he knew that for five years he had had visions of God's power and glimpses of what he might be if only filled with the Holy Spirit.

But was he not already a success? And so for five years he had been struggling against God until Mr. Moody came and had the courage to put his finger upon what others regarded as "success," and quietly to say *"You are a failure! Your work does not count."*

Failure? Yes. With his wonderful eloquence Wilbur Chapman had drawn a splendid congregation from here, there, and everywhere; largely from other churches. But men and women were not being won for Christ; and the members of his church were not stepping out into full surrender and whole-hearted consecration to God.

A failure? At last that eminently "successful" pastor broke down before God and acknowledged his ambition and his pride and yes, his *failure!* God showed him his love of personal ease, and how he was putting love of home before love of God. At length he yielded his *will* to Christ.

He said, "On the 16th day of October, 1892, I came to the place where I said, 'O God, I am willing to be made willing about everything.'" And at once God filled him with "power from on high." His confession is very touching. He says that the change that came into his life is nearly indescribable. "I never knew what it was to love my family before; I question if they ever knew what it was to love me, although we had called ourselves happy in the love of each other. I never knew what it was to study the Bible before, and why should I? For had I not just then found the key? I *never knew what it was to preach* before. 'Old things are passed away' in my Christian experience, and 'behold, all things are become new.'"

After relating this solemn transaction with God, he added, "And if there has been any helpfulness in my ministry, if there has been any ability to win souls, *I know when the change came.*"

Dr. R. A. Torrey, whose ministry was so wonderfully blessed by God, tells the same story. He, too, with all his marvelous gifts, was acknowledged by all as a great "success"; he knew it, and was glad.

One day, however, he was led to choose Matthew 3:11 for his text. "He shall baptize you with the Holy Ghost and with fire." He knelt, as was his custom, to pray for inspiration and guidance; but the Holy Spirit spoke to him *about himself.* His petition was altered, and he cried out, "O God, I do not believe I have that gift myself! I have never been baptized with the Holy Spirit and with fire. And how can I preach it earnestly if I do not possess it? Now, *give me* what I am going to preach upon, as a practical experience for myself, that I may preach upon it as I ought tomorrow night." What followed? God gave him a revelation of himself. He saw himself, he says, "full of vanity, personal ambition, pride, and utterly self-centered."

He tells us that this revelation was "very painful, but very salutary." But God did not stop there. He never shows us our faults merely to throw us into despondency and despair. He gave a glorious revelation of *Himself,* and He sanctified R. A. Torrey.

Mr. Moody tells us of the same experience. When some saintly ladies told him they were praying for him to be filled with the Holy Spirit, he replied a little testily, "Why are you praying for me? Why don't you pray for the people?" He was quite aware that he was a success. Did not people flock to hear him? Were not men crying out, "What must I do to be saved?"

But a venerable and saintly servant of God quietly said to him, after one of his "telling" addresses, "Mr. Moody, the world has yet to see what God can do in and through a man who is wholly surrendered to Him." Moody was startled; almost staggered by the remark, while he mused, "the fire kindles."

God showed him something of his lack of surrender. He laid *his all* upon the altar, and there was no "waiting for the fire"! And who can estimate the wonders wrought by God through that man who failed to get even a small percentage of the educational advantages which so many of us have enjoyed?

Now one can scarcely be surprised, from a human point of view, if such giants as Chapman, Torrey, and Moody regarded themselves as a "success."

The truly amazing thing, however, is that as far as one can judge, the great majority of Christian people seem to be quite content with their spiritual condition and quite happy about the work they are doing.

Christian workers, ordained and lay, go on quite happily without seeing—and often without seeking—definite results. Sunday school teachers and Bible class leaders usually have not the remotest idea where their pupils stand spiritually. The writer has met literally scores of men who have told him that they were Sunday school teachers for months, and even years, before they themselves were converted! No doubt their vicars supposed they were converted men. For the most part no one seems disturbed or distressed over the fact that so many of our choir members and other church officials show no signs of conversion, and often remove themselves from and sometimes oppose a parochial mission.

Everywhere it is taken as a matter of course that the vast majority of our Sunday school children should drift away from all organized religion almost immediately after they leave school. But it is a very rare thing to find any church where the members seem at all concerned about these things, or where there is any sign that they are conscious of failure. Blindly, naively they say, "We are a success."

A conference of leading Christian workers was held some months ago to face these questions. The chairman put the matter forward very lovingly, pointing out the lack of results, lack of fervor, lack of power, and the need of "power from on high." A clergyman—an "evangelist"—who was present, said a little petulantly, "I do not know why you should talk this way. There is nothing wrong with us. A keener, more devoted, more hard-working set of men and women you will not find anywhere."

The very tone in which the remark was made revealed the position of the speaker. "We are a success. We might do better, but we are not failures." Meanwhile, is not the habit of going to the world for "help" on the increase? And often "success" is secured.

During Lent one was asked to preach at a popular church which, I gathered, was the envy of its near neighbors. It was crowded to the doors, as is nearly always the case. The service was fully choral, and the singing on a very high level. Crowds of young people were in evidence everywhere. A spirit of heartiness and comradeship and goodfellowship was conspicuous. The notices revealed the existence of a big and flourishing organization: parochial whist drives, dances, concerts, theatricals were all in full swing, and tickets could be bought at the church doors that Sunday evening! The vicar and his "workers" (!) were all evidently very delighted with the way church affairs were prospering.

Men do not say such things with their lips, but it was expressed as clearly in other ways. "We are a success." Yet one could truthfully write of that church, as was written of another, "Thou sayest, I am rich, and increased with goods, and have need of nothing: and knowest not that thou art wretched, and miserable, and poor, and blind, and naked" (Rev. 3:17). How easy it is to deceive ourselves.

It is easy enough to get the ears of those who are conscious of weakness and failure in their lives, and who are longing for power. But how difficult it is to reach those who quite honestly and sincerely believe themselves to be a success.

"All is quiet at the front," was the message sent by a general again and again during the American Civil War. But a strong reprimand was eventually issued at headquarters. "You are reminded that you are not sent to keep peace, but to drive the enemy back."

Are there not many churches today whose only bulletin is: "All is quiet at the front"? There are no battles because the enemy is not attacked: and while those in the church are smilingly and complacently saying to each other. "Peace! Peace!" the enemy is undermining their position.

This is true of many a church which would reject the introduction of worldly methods.

Today, however, there appears to be an awakening in more than one direction. Those of us who are clergy have been made to think. Our sermons are so poor and ineffective that even so cautious and sane a man as the Archbishop of Canterbury felt obliged to proclaim that fact to the world, at Church Congress. Yet preaching is our great work. We are anointed to preach—just as our Lord Himself was (Luke 4:18) to preach to the unconverted—not to be leaders of the "faithful" in whist-drives and grand dances and Sunday games—things which have, without doubt, been the ruin of many souls. But the remedy is not "burning midnight oil" and miscellaneous study. We must seek "power from on high."

At the yearly meeting of Friends, it was lamented that there was not a sufficient supply of young ministers with "concern" and consecrated ability coming forward. What is lacking is "concern," and that is always absent or weak when we lack the fullness of the Spirit.

At the same time comes the same cry from America. At a great religious conference held in San Francisco the chairman said, "If you can do anything for us in America by sending us someone who *will teach us how to preach*, we shall be greatly indebted, for we cannot do it. We have lost the power of it."

The Anglicans and Scottish Presbyterians have been discussing that remark, and they agreed that it was the note of *urgency* that was lacking in the preaching of today. Listen to their faithful and searching criticism. "The modern preacher has no great anxiety about his people. His message is generally quiet and intelligent, and full of ethical interest, but not urgent. It does not appear to matter very much whether what is being pressed is obeyed at once or not." Can it be God's Holy Spirit who is speaking through such messages?

America cries out, "Send someone to teach us how to

preach." But God has already sent Some One—no other than His Holy Spirit. "Ye shall receive the power of the Holy Spirit coming upon you and *ye shall be witnesses.*"

Fellow preachers, lay and ordained, men and women, we are ambassadors of the living God, "as though God did beseech" men through us! We are children of God, "and if children, then heirs; heirs of God and joint heirs with Christ" (Rom. 8:17). Is it not wonderful? And that declaration occurs in Paul's great chapter on the Holy Spirit. But is this the impression which our congregations get of us? Are our messages Power-Full? Are we preaching a full Christ? Are we preaching the Cross and the atoning blood? Is it a living message we are giving?

In *The Life of Faith* we read lately, "There is one man in America today who is preaching with great power to vast multitudes; in a rare degree he possesses the fight of the evangelist, and I should much like to see the way opened up for him to come to this country." Splendid! But just think for a moment. America calls to us, "Show us how to preach." We call back, "Send us your preacher!"

Meanwhile, God sits in the heavens and looks down upon His children. The Lord Jesus speaks: "All power is given unto me. . . . I am with you" (Matt. 28:18–20).

Christ is with us—*in us,* willing and able to give us *all power.* Why not look to Him for it? John the Baptist, filled with the Holy Spirit from his mother's womb, gave us the same message, "Behold the Lamb of God which taketh away the sin of the world. . . . the same is he who baptizeth with the Holy Ghost" (John 1:29-33). America need not and should not look to us; we ought not to look to America. Let us lift up our eyes to the Lord God Almighty from whom is promised our help, our *Power.*

Where are the servants of God who are willing to allow Him to fill them with the Holy Spirit and to make them Power-Full Christians? "He is able; He is willing," and we do not doubt it, yet we hold back.

Do not let us shirk the question by working harder! We are not lamenting lack of enthusiasm or intensity.

There never was so much work carried on in the name of Christ as there is today: never have there been so many churches, never so many workers, never so much money. But how much of it is spiritual work, done in the power of the Holy Spirit?

What a reversal of opinion there will be one day! Our Lord said, "I, if I be lifted up, will draw." Is our ministry drawing? If not, Christ is not "lifted up" in our work. Popular preachers today are putting Christ down; decrying His claims or denying them. But we can safely leave such to the tender mercies of a suffering Savior, if only we ourselves preach Christ and Him crucified. We can pray for our Lord's defamers. If Saul of Tarsus, an eminent leader of religion, could be converted to Christ, no enemy or false friend of Christ is beyond hope. But God forgive us for venturing to criticize others!

There is only one man of whom I have any right to speak. There was a time in his life when he sincerely and honestly regarded himself as a "success." He had no pride over it, but he certainly was glad about it.

Oh, yes, there were conversions to confirm his belief and add to his complacency (although they were no doubt largely due to the earnest prayers of others!). A success! Then came the still, small voice of God on the first of November a few years back. He saw himself, not as God saw him, for no one could bear that sight and live! But he saw himself *not* a success but "miserable and poor and blind." He also saw possibilities of spiritual power and true success, if only he was absolutely and fully yielded to Christ.

If there has been any success, any men won from darkness to light, any saints led from the valley to the hilltop, it is because the Holy Spirit showed that apparent "success" may be dismal failure.

Now, only the Holy Spirit can do this. Poor fallen people greatly resent the criticism of others. So much so that quite recently in one fashionable West-End church an indignant listener flung a hymn book at the preacher for dwelling upon the evils of dancing!

A few days ago, the man who fancied he was a "success" until God showed him his error met a missionary, who said, "Do you remember staying with us for a few days some twenty years ago? What a marvelous change has come over you! You are an absolutely different man!" What if that dear man had only taken his guest aside and had in a kindly way shown him how he failed to glorify his Lord? Well, probably only indignation and denial and recriminations would have resulted! But when God's Holy Spirit begins to condemn us . . . ! On looking back over the past one can only wonder at the patience and forbearance and long-suffering exhibited by one's fellow workers; and to marvel that God condescended to use one so unworthy. If only this experience may be a warning and help to others! If only we could cease to criticize and commence to pray for "successful" failures.

Thank God, He does use us even when we are failures.

But there is not the outpouring of blessing which ought to be ours. God does grant us results, real spiritual results, even when we are not filled with the Holy Spirit, for He will not allow people to suffer altogether because of the "unworthiness of the minister," or teacher, or speaker.

Do you remember when Moses so grievously failed God at the "rock" in the wilderness? The people were in dire need of water. God told him to "speak" to the rock and water would come forth. But Moses lost his temper over the murmuring people and cried, "Hear now, ye rebels! Must we fetch you water out of this rock? And . . . he *smote the rock twice*" (Num. 20:10—11).

Now Moses was not being lead by the Spirit of God. He was disobeying God. And he seemed to be claiming to be a partner with God in His mighty working. Must we also claim this partnership? This would be pride, presumption, blasphemy. Then he lost his temper, too. Surely God cannot use such a man. Yet notice the result: "And the *water came out abundantly*" (v. 11). God would not allow the people to suffer because of Moses' sin, because he obeyed only partially and in a wrong spirit.

Ah, but God was displeased with Moses and shut him out

of the promised land, taking from his people the one thing he so ardently longed for.

God does not always, cannot always, act in this way. It is an easy thing for God to give people water. But to give the Holy Spirit in converting power is quite another thing. If we refuse to allow Him to fill us with power from on high, we shall be hindering Him from pouring blessing *through us into* countless lives.

Oh, the tragedy of it! We want to see our loved ones, our Sunday school pupils, our congregations truly converted to Christ; and God longs to do it through us, but is thwarted by us unless we are indeed Power-Full Christians. No Christian has any need nor any right to be a failure, provided he is working where God would have him be.

"I *am* a success. But nobody ever says that!" someone replied. Yet every follower of the Lord Jesus *may* say it; and say it reverently, truthfully and humbly. We may not boast about *our* success. But "my soul shall make her boast in the Lord: the humble shall hear thereof, and be glad" (Ps. 34:2). We may cry out, "The Lord hath done great things for us, whereof we are glad."

We may say with Paul, "I can do *all things* through Christ who strengtheneth me."

How, then, may I become a Power-Full Christian?

This question of profound importance must now be answered.

6
How Can I Become a Power-Full Christian?

It must surely be impossible for any Christian man or woman to read the story of Pentecost—when the promised "Power from on high" fell upon all in that Upper Room—without feeling strangely moved, or without longing to get that power.

A bright hope takes possession of the soul and we exclaim, "Is it for me?" And countless thousands in all ages of Christendom have been led to cry out like the woman at Samaria's well. "Lord, Give me this power" ; or like the people who sought out the Savior on the day after the feeding of the 5,000, "Lord, evermore give us this bread [power]" (John 6:34). And many, very many, who are reading these chapters will sadly confess, "Again and again I've longed for power from on high. For many years I have prayed for it. O so earnestly, but it never comes!"

Now, why is this? It is absolutely certain that God desires every child of His to be a Power-Full Christian. It is not the will of your Father that one of His little ones should ever lack power.

Who is the weakest, the poorest, the most worthless Christian? Is it I? Is it you? Gods' command to that person is, "Be filled with the Spirit." One dear saint exclaimed, "There is no aristocracy in the Kingdom of God." Ah, Sir! You are wrong. In his kingdom there is nothing but aristocracy! All His followers are children of God: "heirs of

God and joint- heirs with Christ." Then if I am not a Power-Full Christian the fault is entirely mine. If you are not filled with "power from on high" the fault is entirely yours. There is more: if we are not the recipients of this Holy Power we are grieving God and hindering His work. The greatest sin of the unbeliever is to blaspheme the Holy Spirit; and the greatest fault of the saint is to neglect the Holy Spirit.

But men reply that they are yearning and longing and praying for the fullness of the Holy Spirit, yet that fullness does not come. Are we making the mistake of laying upon Him the responsibility of giving us "power", while He is waiting for us to accept what is given?

God is not calling upon us to make exhaustive efforts, but to submit to Him; not to attempt arduous ascents, but to allow Him to lift us up; not to amass spiritual wealth by exhaustive works, but to open our hands to let the rubbish and waste of this world drop, so that it is possible for those hands to take and to hold Heaven's golden store. Yearning for power, and earnestly praying for it is not receiving it.

A little girl of three had been on a visit to the house of two romping boys, her cousins. On her return she climbed on her father's knees and told him many things. "Father, every night Jack and George say their prayers! They asked God to make them good boys," she added. "That is very nice," was her father's comment. But after a few moments thinking, the little one said, "He hasn't done it yet!"

If we pray day after day, "O Father, fill me, baptize me, with Thy Holy Spirit," and "He has not done it yet," it is for the same reason that those two boys were not "made good," There are some things God cannot do for us without our cooperation. And there are some people who seem unable to learn how to cooperate. On my shelves there are several second-hand books on the work of the Holy Spirit. One of them is by a well known and saintly bishop. It is written in language both simple and clear. On the front page is found the former owner's name and the date, July, 1893. Then underneath is written, "Alas! I am still too stupid to understand all this. April, 1896."

Another book of more ancient date has this inscription on

the last page: "Dec. 9, Sought—," It is quite evident from the long bare line which follows that one word, that the blessing was not "found."

Now, those two pathetic cases are typical of a great multitude of others. What a host of seekers there is today. How earnestly and often one prays that God's gracious, loving, Holy Spirit will make this message so simple, so clear, so plain that even the "stupid" may understand and that everyone who "seeks" shall "find."

A noted Doctor of Divinity said the other day, "It was a great turning point in my ministry when after much thought and study and meditation I became satisfied that the baptism with the Holy Spirit was an experience for today and for me, and set myself about obtaining it. Great blessing came into my life. . . ."

Now it is quite evident that God will not allow this great and blessed and indispensable gift to depend upon any but the simplest and plainest conditions.

What are they? There are seven.

1.

To be a Power-Full Christian, I must first be a Christian. "Power from on high" is only given to true believers on the Lord Jesus Christ. On the morning of the day of Pentecost it fell only on those who believed in the atoning death of Christ, the Son of God on the cross; and in His bodily resurrection, and His ascension into heaven. They at once began to preach Christ crucified, and to promise the gift of the Holy Spirit to all who turned to Him. A notable scene followed. Men were pricked to the heart. They cried out, "Men and brethren, what shall we do?" Peter replied unto them, "Repent, and be baptized every one of you in the name of Jesus Christ for the remission of sins, and ye shall receive the gift of the Holy Ghost" (Acts 2:38).

Those men who crucified our Lord were called upon to "repent"; to change their minds with regard to Him and to accept Him as the Christ, their Messiah and Lord.

So to those who today are crying out, "What shall we do?"

we also would reply, "Have you accepted Jesus Christ by repentance and faith? Are you children of God, not because of your outward baptism or your church membership, but because you have personally and individually yielded yourself to Him and true repentance and faith?" John the Baptist did not go on to speak of the baptism with the Holy Spirit and fire until he had first pointed to the Lamb of God who taketh away the sin of the world.

"Power from on high" only comes upon children of God; those who have already received the Holy Spirit to dwell in their hearts by faith. "Now if any man have not the Spirit of Christ, he is none of his" (Rom. 8:9). It may be that some are reading these chapters hoping to find salvation, crying out, "What must I do to be saved?" Why, that is just what they did on the day of Pentecost! Repent—believe. Be willing to renounce all known sin and look in faith to Jesus Christ, the Lamb of God, to save you. "The blood of Jesus Christ his [God's] Son cleanseth us from all sin" (1 John 1:7).

It was not my intention to enter into this question at all, but merely to refer to the fact that only sons of God may claim power. But a well-to-do city man accosted me a few hours ago. This is what he said, "I have been to church every Sunday for twenty-five years, yet I have never once heard a preacher tell just how a man may become a Christian!"

And there are some reading these lines who do not yet desire to yield their lives to the Lord Jesus. Listen!

During a mission a notice was issued that a special meeting would be held for those who did not desire Christ to save them. Many laughed—some scoffed, but twenty came. The speaker said, "I am sure that if a little thread thin as a cobweb were let down by God from heaven to each of you, not one of you would push it away from you. Although it were almost invisible you would value even the slightest connection between yourself and heaven. Now your coming here tonight is a little link with God. I want it to increase in strength till you are joined to the Lord for ever."

He spoke tenderly and winsomely, and all those twenty men "changed their minds"; repented. They looked in faith to Christ Jesus to save them, and the little thread became a thick bond of love which bound them to Him who loved them and gave Himself for them.

The very fact that you choose to read about the Power-Full Christian reveals the existence of that little thread whose existence the Holy Spirit is ever endeavoring to lead us to recognize.

It is possible for any man however "afar off" to receive Christ by believing on His name, and so to become a son of God this very moment. "For as many as received him to them gave he power to become sons of God, even to them that believe on his name" (John 1:12). This still holds good, and any son of God, at any time, may claim power from on high. "But must we not tarry ten days?" No! Nor even ten hours. At the house of Cornelius "the Holy Spirit fell on all them which heard the word" in the middle of Simon Peter's sermon! (Acts 10:44).

Those Gentile hearers had not yet confessed their faith or uttered their repentance and were not even baptized! But God knew their hearts.

So we may receive the gift at once, if we fulfill God's conditions. A few weeks ago Dr. Northcote Deck said, "We have no need of conventions for the deepening of the spiritual life among the native Christians of the South Sea Islands, for at their conversion, their consecration is so complete that they are at once filled with the Holy Spirit power." "But," someone asks, "are there conditions? Are not God's gifts free for all His children?"

His gifts are absolutely free, requiring nothing but faith; but true faith cannot exist in a false heart.

We believe that failure to obtain the fullness of the Spirit is invariably due to ignorance of God's claims upon us. But what are these claims?

2.

"Power from on high" is not entrusted to every child of God. It is promised to every child, it is offered to every child, yet so often obstacles prevent the acceptance of that great

gift. Sometimes the child of God is not fit to receive the fullness of blessing.

When the Prodigal Son came back home, his father did not invite him to sit down at the table in all rags and filth. It would not have been right or fitting. That loving father could fall on his neck and kiss him in all his rags and wretchedness. And that act of tender love has brought tears to the eyes of many a sinner. It was beautiful. "The portion of love remained" cried a Hindu woman, deeply touched by the story.

But to have the boy at the table in rags! Never! So also there is a communion and a fellowship with God which cannot be enjoyed by anyone who is not clothed with the robe of righteousness. But the father did not expect the Prodigal to provide his own clothes. They were provided for him. And so it is with us; God has made every provision for our holiness. Why did our Lord promise "power"? What was that power to do, to effect? That power is inseparable from the Holy Spirit. It is the power of the Holy Spirit coming upon us. Power is never given to us; this power merely works through us.

What is the great mission of the Holy Spirit? He has only one aim—to glorify Christ. Our Lord said, "He shall glorify me" (John 16:14).

Every act of the Holy Spirit honors the Lord Jesus. Now let us be fully assured of this fact, that if He, the Holy Spirit, comes to dwell in my heart in all the fullness of His power it will be for one purpose only—to glorify Jesus Christ.

Is that my aim? Is my one and only purpose in life just to bring glory to the Lord Jesus? Is that the only reason why I seek power from on high? If it is not, then I shall seek the blessing in vain. Oh, let us be quite clear about this. "Holiness" is not an end in itself! God says to us, "Be ye holy" because He knows that only holiness can witness to His glory. We are called not to be cisterns, but channels. A cistern full of water is absolutely valueless until the water begins to flow.

"He that believeth on Me out of his [inmost being] shall flow rivers of living water" (John 7:38 RV marg.). "We are his workmanship, created in Christ Jesus unto good works" (Eph. 2:10). The fullness of blessing never comes merely to make us happy or holy; God never grants "power from on high" that we may be glorified; that others may talk about us and say what wonderful preachers, or teachers, or personal workers we are. When the beauties of holiness present themselves to our minds, Satan at once begins to tempt us with wrong motives. Many seekers fail to find this inestimable blessing because they are thinking of their own blessedness or peace, or satisfaction, or joy, or usefulness. We are so apt to reflect what a glorious thing it would be for me if I were only a Power-Full Christian! How convincing my life would be; how easy things would become; how quickly difficulties and opposition would be swept out of the way! We may be quite sincere while we are unconsciously quite selfish!

For, after all, self is at the bottom of all these ambitions. Now God cannot trust the fullness of power to selfish people.

Our blessed Master—our example—sanctified Himself in order that others might be sanctified. Listen to His words: "For their sakes I sanctify myself, that they themselves may be sanctified in truth" (John 17:19 RV). And He sanctifies us only that we may help others.

Then others are seeking a blessing which would end in themselves. They are neither preachers nor teachers, nor personal workers. They never speak a word for their Lord and Savior. They even dare to criticize and condemn and make fun of others whose shoes they are not worthy to clean. Yet they will go to a convention and will earnestly seek "power from on high." Are they the folk referred to in a recent letter from one seeking spiritual advice: "The people here flock to meetings for the 'deepening of the spiritual life' when their religion is already so deep that it never comes to the surface?" That dear correspondent hardly realized how such a spirit towards other seekers must be abandoned and conquered before she herself could be blessed!

We must not forget that the promise of "power" is coupled with the willingness to witness: "Ye shall receive power . . . and ye shall be my witnesses" (Acts 1:8). There is a law of nature regarding any gift, which says, "Use it or lose it." In the matter of power from on high we shall seek it in vain if we seek something which is to end in ourselves. Let us then on our knees before God call upon the Holy Spirit to search our hearts through and through and to sift our motives in seeking power. Let Him kill in us all desire to be regarded as saints, all ambition to be spiritual leaders. Let every aim be put aside but that of the Holy Spirit Himself. Jesus Christ said, "He shall glorify me." Ah, how quickly would the "fire" fall if we had but one aim, one consuming, compelling desire that Christ should "be glorified in our mortal bodies." That, and that only! That was the consuming passion in those Pentecostal days.

We see Simon Peter, filled with the Holy Spirit, going forth to preach a sermon which led thousands to Christ. The Lord Jesus was indeed glorified, and no one ever thought of praising Peter or his sermon. "What is this?" they cried; "What is this mighty power?" "It is poured forth from God through Jesus Christ," replied Peter. Yes, it was all Christ and His glory. Later on he exclaims, "Why look ye so earnestly on us, as though by our own power or holiness we had made this man to walk? God . . . hath glorified his Son Jesus. . . . And his name through faith in his name hath made this man strong" (Acts 3:12–16 RV)

Stephen was also filled with the Holy Spirit. He was not chosen by the Church to preach. He was selected to distribute alms to the poor, while the Apostles prayed and preached (Acts 6:4). He was willing to labor in the background and God could fill him with the Holy Spirit. His witness, however, did not end with almsgiving (as perhaps some of ours does?). He, too, preached a sermon. But, full of the Holy Spirit and power as he was, we do not hear of a single convert. Yet the Lord Jesus was glorified just as much by that sermon as by Simon Peter's. For it was a "Holy Spirit sermon."

Instead of rejoicing over converts, Stephen was led forth and stoned to death! And the Lord Jesus was glorified.

"What!" you exclaim, "How?" "Thou knowest not now, but

thou shalt know hereafter." Many of us think that Saul of Tarsus owed his conversion to Stephen.

No, not to his sermon; that only caused Saul to gnash his teeth in anger. But the very glory of God shone forth in the Christ-like way in which Stephen endured opposition, persecution, martyrdom, death. Why even his face shone like that of an angel!

Fellow-Christian, face the question fairly. Are you truly seeking "power from on high"? Very well, thank God.

But if you knew that to become a Power-Full Christian would mean your being persecuted, despised and stoned to death for the glory of God, would you still eagerly press forward for the gift? Let us be quite frank about it. Do self, self-seeking, self-appraisement, and self-glorification enter into the question? Am I willing to face and endure social ostracism and ridicule, even from professing Christians? We only say face the question. It is not right for us to doubt God's power by constantly asking ourselves, "Should I deny my Lord, or fail, or fall if threatened with this or that?"

The only point is this: Is it my desire to glorify my Lord? If the coming of the Holy Spirit in all His fullness should reveal to me that God would have me glorify Him in missions overseas, am I willing to go? If "fullness of blessing" depends upon my giving up doubtful pleasure or harmful "friends" am I willing to let them go? God's glory!

Can we honestly look into the face of our adorable Lord and say, "O Lord, evermore give me this power, and I will follow Thee wherever Thou leadest me, and wilt do anything Thou shalt ask of me, if only Thou mayest be glorified in me, and through me"?

God's will.

Nothing less.

Nothing else.

Nothing more!

A girl in a factory in the South of England recently sought "power from on high" for God's glory. Alone in the work-shop, she stood for Christ. The "power" was seen and felt and resented by the other girls.

But she stood firm, believing that the Lord Jesus was

being glorified. After much opposition and petty persecution, the day came when matters were brought to a climax. "You profess to follow Jesus Christ," cried some of the girls, "and you shall follow Him. You too shall be crucified." They seized her and bound her with out-stretched arms to her bench; and pelted her with pieces of work. "Crucified with Christ, nevertheless I live, yet not I, but Christ liveth in me."

Yes, that "crucifixion" gave her the opportunity to glorify Christ. How easily self could have seized the situation with "righteous indignation"; "dignified" protest to the foreman, or the management; scathing rebuke to the miscreants."

No! She could be trusted with power. The meekness and sweetness and holy joy with which she took her persecution brought some of those rough factory hands to the Savior, "who his own self bare our sins in his own body on the tree . . . by whose stripes ye were healed" (1 Peter 2:24).

Can we not be willing to share the "fellowship of his sufferings" if only by our Christ-like endurance of "stripes" we may glorify Him? The question really comes down to this: Can we be trusted with power? We might alter a well-known chorus and sing:

> Can you be trusted with power?
> Can you be trusted with power?
> Christ is waiting for you to be loyal and true
> And there is no end to the good you may do,
> If you can be trusted with power.

St. Francis of Assisi was asked, late in life, how it was he had been able to accomplish so much for God.

"This may be why God has blessed my efforts," he replied. "The Lord looked down from heaven and said, 'Where can I find the weakest, the littlest, the poorest man on the face of the earth?' Then He saw me and said, 'Now I have found him, I will work through him, for he will not be proud of it. He will realize that I am only using him because of his littleness and insignificance.'"

It seems to me that the whole point is this. Am I weak enough for God to empower? Am I small enough for God to empower? Am I small enough to be "of no reputation," so that Christ in me may be all in all? Our Lord Jesus Christ "emptied Himself" of His glory when He came to reveal God to us; we have to do the same. If only we could come to the place where we have no thought of what we can do for God, but be full of the thought of what God can do through us, when we are wholly yielded to Him! When anyone comes to the place where he is able to say to his Lord and Master, "Lord Jesus, where Thou wilt, what Thou wilt, as Thou wilt," that one is not far from becoming a Power-Full Christian.

It is not an extraordinary thing that any believer should be afraid of God's will? He is our loving Heavenly Father, who has promised that "no good thing will he withhold from them that walk uprightly" (Ps. 84:11). And there is no thing so "good" as God's will. It is good and perfect; but is it acceptable? (Rom. 12:2).

Have you ever thought what an astonishing inspiration there is in making the resolve, "Henceforth in all I think, and say, and do, I will put Christ's glory first"? Before going one further step on life's journey make that your resolve; or renew that resolve. Let the first thought each day be, "I am given another day in which to bring glory to Christ, in little things as well as in great." Let the first words each day be "To me to live is Christ." Let the frequent prayer each day be, "Lord, glorify Thy name!" Let the constant thought be the trustful, joyous recollection, "The Lord Jesus is being glorified in my body." Let us ever be on the watch for opportunities to bring glory to our Blessed Savior.

Ever be on your watchtower. Hour after hour glorious chances are given us. Oh, that we may see them and seize them.

When disappointment, or trouble, or sorrow, or pain comes—when opposition, unkindness, sarcasm, hatred or persecution meets us, may the first thought be, "How can I make this reflect His glory?"

Live each day in that spirit, and you will find every day a glorious and thrilling adventure for Christ. Sweet and holy communion with the indwelling Christ will become a habit.

We shall not need to pray—

> Lord Jesus make Thyself to me
> A living, bright reality.

We shall know that "He is nearer than hands and feet." There is no simpler way to holy living than this. When Christ's glory is our aim we shall count it all joy when we fall into manifold temptations (James 1:2).

When Christ's glory is our aim we shall count it all joy when people speak to us abusively, persecute us, and say things against us, falsely, because of Christ—for it provides us with a chance of glorifying our Lord.

Have you noticed that *two* of our Lord's "Blessings" are given to those who are persecuted? Our Lord calls upon all such "to rejoice and be exceeding glad" (Matt. 5:10—12).

O let us all live this life of adventure for Christ. Are you noted for your hot temper, your biting tongue, your snappy answers? Then "rejoice and be exceeding glad" in surprising your friends by showing the Spirit of Christ! They will recognize it at once as not being your spirit, but due to Divine Power dwelling within.

"Ah, but I am so weak!" you say. Then thank God for it. He has said, "My grace is sufficient for thee; for my strength is made perfect in weakness." Let us say with Paul, "most gladly therefore will I rather glory in my weaknesses, that the Power [dynamis] of Christ may rest upon me"—Greek, "spread a tabernacle over me" (2 Cor. 12:9).

Compare John 1:14 RV: the words "rest"—quoted above, and "dwelt" (in John 1:14) are the same Greek verb. Men will "behold Christ's glory" in us too.

It is an amazing thing that God should choose me to be the instrument of revealing His glory. But He has done it! And He has chosen you. Let us not disappoint Him.

O God, come what may, let me glorify the Lord Jesus all day and every day.

Strange to say, we may dishonor Christ even in the way in which we seek to be Power-Full Christians!

Mr. Trumbull has brought this point out so forcibly in a short editorial in the *Sunday School Times* that we venture to repeat the illustration he gave.

He says, "To be satisfied with the Lord Jesus Himself is the secret of victory in the life, and power in service. God the Father is completely satisfied with His beloved Son. And God's goal for us is that we shall be perfectly satisfied with our Savior and Lord—with all He is to us, and with what He is doing for us. A consecrated Christian woman who was doing a fine work in Bible teaching became much dissatisfied as she began to seek for a certain experience of the baptism of the Holy Spirit. She came for help to a Christian minister, who told her the trouble was that she was not satisfied with Jesus Christ. 'Yes, of course I am satisfied with the Lord Jesus, but—' 'Now wait,' the minister said, 'if you really know what it means to be satisfied with Jesus, there will be no "buts" to follow that confession. You want something besides Jesus. What is it you want?' 'I want power!' 'What do you want power for?' 'For the sake of the girls I teach.' 'Do you want them to get this experience you speak of?' 'No, I would never say a word to them about that. I want them to know Christ in a personal way.'

" 'Do you not think that the greatest power you can use is to let them see how completely Christ satisfied your own heart and meets your needs, instead of letting them see you worried and unsatisfied because you have not had a certain experience?' 'But I have not told them I am troubled!' An intimate friend who was sitting with her gently reminded her that the girls knew it—her lack of peace was written in her face. It is good to hunger after God's power in life; to be satisfied with what the Lord Jesus is doing does not mean to be satisfied with what He is not doing. But if we are hungry and dissatisfied let us not strive and strain after some "experience"; let us come in humble surrender to Him, and confess 'all that I want is in Jesus: He satisfies.' "We must, indeed, be very careful how we seek to be filled with the Holy Spirit. Our dissatisfaction must be wholly with ourselves and not with our adorable Lord and Master. For it is still true that "If we worry we do not trust; and if we trust we do not worry." And, after all, power is simply manifesting the glory of Christ, as we have pointed out before. Oh, that the life of Jesus might be ever made manifest—that is, visible—in our body! (2 Cor. 4:10).

3.

The Bible tells us that God gives the Holy Spirit "to them that obey him" (Acts 5:32). What about sin? Now our motive in seeking power from on high may be right while our personal life is wrong in some directions. We may desire nothing but God's glory and yet be disobedient in some apparently little thing, which we try not to think of.

We may be quite sure that the power we receive from God never exceeds the obedience we render to God. When we can honestly say to God "All that thou commandest I will do," then the Heavenly Father says to us, "All that I have is thine."

St. Augustine says, "In the will of God carried out by man God finds a home."

Obedience! Christians often say to themselves and to others. "It is true I go here and go there, but I always take Jesus Christ with me." Is that obeying Christ, or making Christ obey us?

One Sunday evening a clergyman preached on the Holy Spirit and His leadership. On the following Monday he met one of the Sunday school teachers going to a dance. As is invariably the case, that Christian felt she ought to make some excuse.

"It's true I go to dances, but I always take the Holy Spirit with me," said she. "Ah!" replied the vicar, "and how long is it since the Holy Spirit asked you to lead Him?"

We can be no man's conscience. Each one must rely upon the Holy Spirit for guidance. But if there is any practice or any amusement about which most believers find it necessary to make excuses, or apologies or explanations would it not be well to forsake that practice? So we come to the question of sin.

Is there anything in the life which we know to be unholy, unclean, or unworthy? Is there any worldliness, or laxity of conduct or doubtful indulgence, or any root of bitterness which hinders the coming of the blessing?

We may say, "is it not a little thing?" But the smallest willful sin is sufficient to keep us back from power.

Surely we know that God's Holy Spirit and man's sin cannot live together peaceably? They may both be in the same heart, but they cannot both reign there. For the "flesh" (i.e., self) must always "lust against the spirit." You may ask, "What is sin?" That we may safely leave the Holy Spirit to show us. But may I give you a very simple test? How many of us have felt at family prayers that we cannot read a certain passage or offer some prayer because it condemns so clearly our own recent behavior? Ah! how many of us feel guilty. That is the Holy Spirit convicting us of sin.

A deeply honored missionary felt led to confess her own past failures at a conference this year. She pointed out the three most prevalent sins of missionaries (people who have given up so much for Christ: home, friends, prospects, comforts, ease, and who risk health and often life itself for Christ's sake.) The most deadly sins are, (1) Evil speaking; (2) Selfishness; and (3) Pride. And if our devoted and self-denying missionaries suffer thus, are we at home liable to escape?

Of evil speaking she said, "For sheer misery-producing power on a mission station, I have never seen anything like it. How it wrecks the unity, and splits up friends, and does the most awful havoc." She confessed that she only told her husband (poor man!) of other people's faults. God showed her this was wrong, and she said, "Lord, it shall go." But the habit was too deep-rooted. she prayed to God for "a new mouth and a new mind that did not want to do it." And God gave it to her, and it was "the most extraordinary miracle you ever saw", as she explains it. God stopped this sin in her life.

God grants every one of us power to cease from evil speaking. Do not pass this on to another. Are you guilty? Think it over. For this sin is preeminently satanic. It was the first sin that the devil exhibited to man: Satan spoke evil of God (Gen. 3:4—5), and the tragic thing is that man believed the Father of Lies rather than his Creator and

Benefactor! And Satan has been an accuser of the brethren ever since (Rev. 12:10).

He delights to make "serpents" of you and me by putting a sting in our tongue and adders' poison under our lips (Ps. 140:3). He started with Adam and Eve: Adam blamed Eve, and Eve blamed the serpent. With many of us the first step towards becoming a Power-Full Christian will be a cleansed tongue.

Oh, may God from this very moment give us the will and the power to cease from being accusers of the brethren.

But we trust that for most of us our sins consist of misuse of rightful things. Putting loved ones before our Lord; failing really to love those whom we work with and for similar shortcomings. It is quite certain that the rivers of living water which our Savior says shall flow out of our innermost being, can only flow out of clean vessels.

Am I a clean channel? Moody has said many, many times, "God does not seek silver vessels, and He does not require gold ones for His service, but He must have clean ones." What treasures God can store even in earthen vessels! This cleansing can come only to those who are fully surrendered to God—the yielding of the body which is so often the instrument of sin. The heart is so deceptive. It is "deceitful above all things and desperately wicked; who can know it?" (Jer. 17:9). Only the blessed Holy Spirit, who graciously searches that heart (Rom. 8:27). He knows its wickedness and He knows how to help all our "infirmities."

Let us not be hurried or superficial in our self-examination. We must get alone with God and ask Him to reveal to us our sinfulness. We must cry, "Search me, O God, and know my heart: try me, and know my thoughts. And see if there be any wicked way in me, and lead me in the way everlasting" (Ps. 139:23—24).

God's Holy Spirit will then show us what is wrong. And then? Is it really possible for me to cling to some sinful or even doubtful habit which brings me an occasional and fleeting satisfaction, although I know it robs me of fullness of joy as a blessed and constant experience, and robs me of that "power from on high" without which my service and my witness are valueless? Yes, incredible as it sounds, it is possible. And many who will read these lines are allowing some trivial, despicable "little" sin to keep them out of this incomparable blessing. "Your iniquities have separated between you and your God, and your sins have hid his face from you, that He will not hear" (Isa. 59:2). When you plead for "power from on high" and all its treasures of blessing, "your iniquities have turned away these things, and your sins have withholden good things from you" (Jer. 5:25). "I beseech you—I beseech you therefore, brethren, by the mercies of God, to present all faculties to him as a living and holy sacrifice acceptable to him" (Rom. 12:1 see Weymouth).

Oh, the joy and delight that follow such full surrender! Let not one of us allow a little selfishness, pride, temper, misunderstanding, envy, jealousy, the desire to criticize and condemn others, to remain in our hearts. This will cause great grief to God and pain to our friends; and it will spoil our own lives, our witness, and our usefulness as Christians.

If God's Holy Spirit shows us anything that is wrong or doubtful we must be willing to put it away at once. And this must be done out of love for Christ, and not as a bargain in order to receive "power," or we become dangerously near to meriting the rebuke which Simon Magus received (Acts 8:18–24). I say we must be willing; for in the first place it is always a matter of the will, the surrendering of the will to God. "Wilt thou be made whole?" When there is a "will to obey," acts of obedience follow.

At a convention recently held in North India, a missionary received a very wonderful and definite enduement of power. He said to a friend sometime after, "I was not the man of power I meant to be when I first came out, and I did not see how I could get out of the drift. But I faced things and then I told God I was willing; and you know the rest!"

Now God will do for every one of us what He did for that missionary. He is watching us, pleading with us by His "mercies" and His warnings, because He longs to bless us in a more wonderful way than ever before.

Are we willing for Him to do so?

We must ever bear in mind that we are not seeking some impersonal power; some electric shock, or thrill, or state of ecstasy. We are seeking a fuller knowledge of a Person, a deep communion with a Person, a greater love for a Person, to be brought absolutely and wholly under the control of a Person. And that Person is the Holy Spirit of God, Who loves us with a love that passes all understanding.

It is He, the Comforter, the Advocate, the Great Intercessor who brings the "power from on high." He *is* the power. And He is already dwelling in our hearts and only waits to be given complete control over our lives. He knows that we are Power-Full only when we are entirely in His hands to speak, live, go, and act just as He desires.

Dan Crawford says that the Negro of Central Africa translates the verse, "My times are in thy hands" (Ps. 31:15), "in the gorgeous words": "All my life's why's, and when's, and where's and wherefore's are in Thy hands." And when we are content to have it so, we are Power-Full Christians.

So then this "power" is nothing else but the Blessed Holy Spirit working in our hearts and through our lives.

It may help us to think over this fact. My greatest friend the Holy Spirit of God dwells within my heart. He is a guest there. He transforms my heart and body into a "temple" (1 Cor. 6:19). Note that it is not only in my heart that He dwells. "Know ye not that your body is the temple of the Holy Ghost which is in you . . . and ye are not your own?" (1 Cor. 6:19).

A convert in Japan put the whole thing very simply and clearly. He had betrayed a trust and had fled from his native town, determined to commit suicide. Tired out with traveling he entered a Gospel tent, and was convicted of sin. Long after midnight he found peace with God. Four days later, he said to missionary, "How can I help but believe in the Resurrection of Christ when He has risen in my heart?" Then he added, "My body is a kind of temple of Christ's, so I must not defile it by committing sin. If I sin, the Lord within will be blamed for it." This man up till four days previously had no knowledge whatever of Christian truth, nor had these deeper things of God been preached from the platform. His teacher could have been none other but the Holy Spirit dwelling in him. Why is it then that *we* are so slow to learn these things?

Now, let us think of our Guest. What does a dear friend expect as a matter of course when he is a guest in our home? He knows that he has our friendship and our love but he also expects our companionship and our attention. He would be very surprised if he were ignored, if only occasionally.

We give much thought to the comfort of our guest. We do nothing to displease him. We avoid offering him food which we know he dislikes, and we exclude people who would be distasteful to him. We provide for him our best and earnestly desire that he should feel at home. Now have we ever thought of the Holy Spirit as a Guest?

How strange it is that among those who pray for the fullness of the Holy Spirit, so few trouble to sit down—or kneel down—and count the cost. Possibly the secret of the Power-Full Christian may be summed up in this: He is one who treats the Holy Spirit as the all-loving, all-powerful Guest of his heart. If only we were as careful about His interests and wishes and commands as we are for those of an earthly guest! It is astonishing how much time we can give to a visitor in our home without neglecting our ordinary duties. And it is possible to treat our Heavenly Guest in the same way; possible to always be conscious of His indwelling; possible to have communion and fellowship with Him all the day long. Occasionally we can get away to the inner chamber to be alone with Him; but we can at all times have the joy of the consciousness of His indwelling.

Then there is the other side of the question. We not only give, but we get. A wise guest is frequently confided in and consulted. We tell him of our domestic troubles and business difficulties, and he solves many of our perplexities for us. His counsel often corrects a hasty judgment and prevents an angry or unkind reply, while his advice is often very greatly to our advantage and interests. But our Heavenly Guest, the gracious, loving Holy Spirit, comes only to give. True it is that He asks for our love and our worship. But He is the Paraclete—The Advocate—One who comes alongside to help. He comes to dwell in our hearts to guide us into all truth; to reveal to us the Father.

He comes to "grant you according to the riches of his glory, to be strengthened with might, by his Spirit in the inner man; that Christ may dwell in your hearts by faith; that ye . . . may . . . know the love of Christ, which passeth knowledge, that ye might be filled with all the fullness of God" (Eph. 3: 16–19).

There He is, within us, longing to give these spiritual gifts to us and yet so many of us, even Christian people refuse them! He is surely saying to some of us, "All day long I have stretched forth my Hands unto a disobedient and gainsaying people" (Rom. 10:21)—hands full of the "riches of his glory." It seems incredible that any should refuse them.

Ah! What a Guest He is! No problem is too deep for Him; no difficulty too great. Nothing which concerns us is outside His interest and His care. He rejoices to be consulted, and it always brings rejoicings to us when we obey.

We shall fail every time we refuse to allow Him to control. Yet how often can we say with full assurance, "It seemed good to the Holy Spirit and to us"? (Acts 15:28).

Dr. Campbell Morgan says: "God has not promised to come and help men to do His work. This is no idle play upon words; the difference is radical." Just as much as we value and reckon upon "the grace of our Lord Jesus Christ, and the love of God," so are we to value and profit by "the fellowship [communion] of the Holy Spirit."

And real communion is not possible unless there is complete obedience on our part. The Holy Spirit who dwells within us claims and expects to have full control over our lives.

There must be no divided allegiance. John Bunyan brings this out in his inimitable way. You will remember how Diabolus proposes through his ambassador, Mr. Loth-to-Stoop again said, "Sir, behold the condescension of my master! He says he will be content if he can have some place assigned to him in Mansoul as a place to live in privately; and you shall be Lord of all the rest!" Ah! how many are robbed of the fullness of blessing and power because they consent to this. Secretly, in their inmost beings is some "little" space where Satan is allowed to dwell "privately." But the Lord Jesus demands that He shall be the only guest in our hearts. Even "self" must stand aside and allow Him absolute dominion.

Is it too much to ask that each of us should agree to this? Emmanuel's reply was this, "All that the Father giveth me shall come to me, and of all that he giveth me I will lose nothing, no, not a hoof, or a hair. I will not, therefore, grant Diabolus, no, not the least corner in Mansoul to dwell in. I will have it all to myself."

We cannot be Power-Full Christians until we yield ourselves, our souls and our bodies entirely to the indwelling Holy Spirit. What joy, what peace, what power comes to the man who honestly says, "Lord Jesus, Thou shalt have me all to Thyself."

> Made for Thyself, O god!
> Made for Thy love, Thy service, Thy delight:
> Made to show forth Thy wisdom, grace, and might.
> Made for Thy praise Whom veiled Archangels laud.

O strange and glorious thought that we may be a joy to God! We are not our own. We are bought with a price. We are His. And He must be Master over His own house, whose house we are (Heb. 3:6): not only as a welcome and privileged Guest, while we "keep the keys and the care."

An evangelist related that he asked a business man this question, "How long would you keep a man in your employ if you knew that he was half for you and half for your rival?" "I should keep him only till I found it out!" was the quick reply. Then turning to his desk he took out the agreement which his employees made with the firm. That agreement was practically this: "All my strength and all my influence are yours." "When a man is willing to sign that contract," he said "then we give him permission to use our name. We could not give him that privilege if we cannot control him." And that is the attitude of God the Holy Spirit. He earnestly desires to make an agreement with us. His Name is at our disposal. His power is at our disposal. God's "riches in glory in Christ Jesus" are at our disposal, if only we are willing to present—to yield to Him all we have, all we are: our talents, our powers, our plans, our life.

But whatever we give Him has no value unless we first give Him our wills in loving and loyal allegiance. Many give God service, self-sacrificing and devoted service, but do not yield themselves.

Consider Jesus. All power, wisdom, knowledge, love, peace, and joy are His. He always knows what is best for us. He always knows the right course to take and the right thing to say and do. He has never erred in judgment; never made a mistake. He is the Guest of our hearts asking to be allowed to guide us into all truth. We can say, as Christ said, "He that sent me is with me; He hath not left me alone." But can we say, "I do always the things that are pleasing to Him"? (John 8:29 RV).

What a Guest! He is able to make all grace to abound toward us. He "is able to do exceedingly abundantly above all that we ask or think, according to the power that worketh in us" (Eph. 3:20). What amazing mistakes we make to resist Him, to disobey Him!

By the wondrous mercies of God, I beseech you, brethren, "to present your bodies a living sacrifice, holy, acceptable [well-pleasing], to God which is your reasonable service" (Rom. 12:1 RV).

5.

No man lives to himself. We cannot be Power-Full Christians if we are wrong in our relationships to others; if there is any "root of bitterness" in us. We must resolutely face this question.

Our Lord on His Resurrection Day could not appear to the Apostolic Band and the faithful women of His company until peace and unity dwelt among them. He appears to have spent the whole day in bringing together His divided followers. They were human; and "the Holy Spirit was not yet given." So we can scarcely be surprised if they felt indignant with Simon Peter for denying our Lord with oaths and curses; or if the women despised him for it; and if Peter felt himself not only under a cloud but no longer a disciple. Then Clopas and his friend (his wife?) seemed to have given up all hope and were apparently leaving the cause of Christ. For had not the "cause" collapsed with His death? They had to be brought back; not by compulsion, not by command, but by a further and gracious revelation of Himself and His love.

Mary Magdalene, who "loved most because forgiven most"—for had not our Lord cast seven devils out of her?—must have felt very indignant with Simon Peter; for love knows no fear and is apt to despise fear shown by others. So she is chosen by our Lord to tell Peter of His resurrection and His forgiveness. The Angel said, "Go, tell his disciples and Peter. . . ." (Mark 16:7 RV). The Angel could have told Peter himself, but Mary had to learn a lesson. What a revelation of love! Christ had forgiven her all her sins; we cannot believe that God would allow seven devils to possess anyone whose life did not tend to encourage devil possession. And He had evidently forgiven Simon Peter. How then could Mary Magdalene withhold forgiveness from poor Simon? So once more love fills her heart and she turns to obey the angelic command. It was then and only then that the Blessed Lord appears to her.

Believe me, our vision of the Risen and Ascended Lord will be dimmed, or blurred, or destroyed if we do not "love our brother also," however much he may have sinned against God and against us.

At any rate, it was not until our Lord had brought reconciliation to all the Apostles and the women of the company that He appeared to the assembled body of the faithful. Then, and only then, could He say, "Peace be unto you . . . And when he had said this, he breathed on them, and saith unto them, 'Receive ye the Holy Ghost'" (John 20:21–22 RV).

It was the same at Pentecost. It was not until they were all with one accord in one place that the Holy Spirit fell upon them. Personally I do not believe it is possible for a person to be endued with "power from on high" unless he is at peace with others as well as with God. "Follow peace with all men" is a command which precedes "and holiness, without which no man shall see the Lord" (Heb. 12:14). To harbor any spirit of hatred or disgust or dislike towards others will most certainly prevent the reception of power. As far as in us lieth we are to live peaceably with all men.

We must not make exceptions for those who err concerning the faith. "Religious"—so called—controversy can be very bitter. It ought not to be so. We may hate the false teaching of those church dignitaries who, being prominent members of the visible Church, attack our Lord and His claims and His Book; but we must love them. Paul's counsel is clear. "I beseech you, brethren, mark them which cause divisions and offenses contrary to the doctrine which ye have learned; and avoid them. For they that are such serve not our Lord Jesus Christ" (Rom. 16:17–18).

We are to pray for them. Prayer is a great antidote to hate. Nothing but a spirit of love must fill the heart. "Seeing ye have purified your souls in obeying the truth through the Spirit unto unfeigned love of the brethren, see that ye love one another with a pure heart fervently" (1 Peter 1:22).

This is of the utmost importance. Among earnest Christian workers there is so much jealousy, petulance, idle gossip about each other, unkind criticism, spreading of evil reports, exaggerating little slips of word or deed, imputing wrong motives. All these are signs of unlove; and all or any of these hinder the blessed Holy Spirit from dwelling within in all His fullness.

The writer once met a man who seemed to be absolutely devoted to the Lord Jesus; a man of prayer and a man whose life was full of good works. He was apparently a holy and humble man of heart who desired only the glory of God. And yet—? There was nothing apparently wrong and very much to admire. Yet one felt very much like Paul when he met those Ephesian Christians and said, "Did ye receive the Holy Ghost when ye believed?" (Acts 19:2 RV). One day in a moment of confidence my friend betrayed his secret. He was harboring a grudge against one who had been his greatest friend. This led to deceit and many an acted lie. Now of what use was it for the devoted man, trying to probe the secrets of the Victorious Life? Of what use was it for him to spend hours on his knees pleading for the fullness of the Holy Spirit?

The hindrance to the blessing was there in his own heart and attitude. The Holy Spirit was striving with him instead of working through him in mighty power. Verily God was saying in sorrow once again, "Your sins have withholden good things from you" (Jer. 5:25).

That little thing—or rather sin—is a cloud in the sky which veils the glory of the Lord. Indeed, all of us have been guilty of such sins, and each of us must bear patiently with, and very tenderly with, others who fail.

Many of us who serve the Lord Jesus still need to "get right with God" by getting right with our fellow workers.

Peter in writing to the "elect" (see 1 Peter 1:1 RV) finds it necessary to quote Psalm 34:12. "He that would love life and see good days, let him refrain his tongue from evil, and his lips that they speak no guile. . . . Let him seek peace and pursue it" (1 Peter 3:10—11 RV). And we find it still necessary to repeat this admonition even to the "elect."

May God help every one of us to let this "hindrance to power" drop out of our lives.

6.

This God-given, Father-promised power does not fall upon us all at once. It may be that there are still subtle hindrances in the way. There are three very common ones. We may be waiting for proofs that the power has come; or we may not be really very desirous of becoming Power-Full Christians; or we may have no real wish to be fellow workers with Christ in His vineyard.

Let us take these three in turn and explain just what we mean.

1. We may be marking out the channel in which we expect God's power to flow. That is to say, we may have formed

wrong ideas as to how the power of the Holy Spirit should manifest itself. Are we expecting a "speaking in tongues," or thrills, or ecstasies, or some other overwhelming proof that the power has fallen upon us? We feel sure that this is inexpedient, if not fatal.

Remember that we can never anticipate just how God will work. But we can be sure of this; He always has better things for those who obey Him than they plan for themselves.

Those 120 disciples in the Upper Room simply waited—and doubtless prayed—for the Holy Spirit. They certainly had not the vaguest notion how this "power from on high" would make itself felt and known. So much power had already;y been granted them, and so many privileges bestowed on them, that it was beyond their ability to fathom or foretell the content of Christ's promise. What further "power" could there be? No doubt they eagerly discussed the words of John the Baptist, "He shall baptize you with the Holy Spirit and with fire." But even what that meant none could guess.

They knew that the Comforter—the Spirit of truth—would illuminate their minds and aid their memories: would lead them into all truth; would testify of the Lord Jesus Christ and would glorify Him. They had been told that He would take of the things of Christ and show them to all believers; would dwell in them and make them know that Christ was in the Father and they were in Christ, and Christ in them. But apart from this they were just content to wait upon God and leave this wondrous manifestation to work in whatever way seemed fit to Him.

> Lord, we ask it, hardly knowing
> What this wondrous gift may be:
> Yet fulfil to overflowing,
> Thy great meaning let us see.

2. Yet those ten days of waiting must have made them intensely desire and long for the promise of the Father.

That delay of ten days also allowed Jerusalem to become full of visitors to the Feast. As those disciples, in the intervals between their seasons of prayer, were jostled by people from "every nation under heaven" they must have recalled their Master's command, "Go ye into all the world" (Mark 16:15). "Go ye, therefore, and make disciples of all the nations" (Matt. 28:19 RV).

They must have felt unfit, unprepared, and unequipped for such a task. This must have deepened their sense of need and intensified their desire for "power from on high."

Now we scarcely think that God will bestow this "power" upon us unless we have a deep sense of need and unless we desire with all our heart to be empowered by the Holy Spirit. But yearning desire is not enough. There must be faith.

In writing to the Galatians Paul said, ". . . that we might receive the promise of the Spirit through faith" (Gal. 3:14). He does not say "receive the Spirit through faith"; that would be unscriptural for he is writing to Christians who as believers already possess the Holy Spirit. He dwells in us to abide with us for ever. We are to receive the promise by faith. Have we reached the position of those disciples just before Pentecost? They were very deeply attached to the Savior. They had given up all to follow Him. Their hearts were entirely occupied with the Lord Jesus. Is it so with us? Is He to us "altogether lovely and the fairest of ten thousand?" Have we "forsaken all"? Are we truly separate from the world? Or are we going to God for power while going to the "world" for pleasure? "Then shall ye seek me and find me, when ye shall search for me with all your heart."

These disciples had come to an end of themselves. Their self-importance and self-reliance had gone. Once they practically cried, "We are a success! Even the devils are subject to us." Now they had come to realize that without this enduement of power from on high they are useless and could be nothing but failures. Have we, too, reached this point? For this gift does not come unsought. The promise is: "I will pour my spirit upon thy seed" (Isa. 44:3).

Are we indeed thirsty? Are our souls "athirst for God, even for the living God"?

3. Then there is the danger of thinking that God will bless us, simply that we may be blessed. No—He bestows His gifts

in order that others may be blessed through us. Only a witnessing Christian can be a Power-Full Christian. Are we workers in His vineyard? Or rather, are we willing to work for our blessed Master in any sphere, in any place, in any way? "On my servants [Greek—'bondmen'] and on my handmaidens [Greek—'bondmaidens'] . . . will I pour forth of my spirit" (Acts 2:18 RV).

Can we honestly say (1) I make no conditions as to how the blessing shall come. (2) With all my very being I yearn for power from on high. (3) I am willing to witness and to work as the Holy Spirit shall lead me. Then there remains only one other step—just to *claim* the "promise of the Father."

7.

If after careful and prayerful meditation we have fulfilled the conditions we have outlined, *then we can with confidence CLAIM the fullness of the Spirit.*

Mr. McConkey tersely says:

> Do not await it—believe it.
> Do not expect it—accept it.
> Do not seek for it—recognize it.
> Do not inspect your emotions; but expect His motions.

My firm conviction is that many earnest people get to this point where nothing remains for them to do but just hold out the empty hand of faith and receive (I do not even say "take," which implies some effort on our part), receive "power from on high," and then fail to do so.

A noted evangelist, speaking in London, said that his heart was burdened for the men of a city in which he was working. He called together a few Christian men of his church and told them of a plan he had in mind. He pointed out that plans and organization were useless without the "infilling of the Holy Spirit." As he spoke upon this matter he noticed a young man who had had very little education pick up his hat and walk out. On leaving the hall later on, the evangelist heard a voice in another room. There he found this young man literally on his face before God. He was still praying, "O God," said he, "I implore Thee for this 'power from on high.'" Then there was silence. "O Father," he went on, "I will give up every known sin if only I can witness for Thee." Again there was silence, as if he was reviewing his past life. "Yes—I will give that up," he began again, "Yes, they shall go." Then he rose from his knees and looking up to heaven said, "And now, Father, I claim the blessing."

Then he became aware of his pastor's presence and with a radiant face turned and seized the evangelist's hand and said, "I have received Him! I have received Him!"

His whole life was transformed. And in spite of his ignorance and lack of education, in a few months he was the means by which sixty men were led to Christ as their Savior.

Every fully yielded believer may receive "power from on high" in the same way. By repentance and faith any sinner may be saved. By repentance and faith any believer may be sanctified and become a Power-Full Christian.

One who for many years had been praying for the fullness of the Holy Spirit was amazed when this was pointed out to her. "But can I claim power from on high in the same way as I claimed forgiveness of my sins?" she asked in astonishment. "Assuredly you can, if you have fulfilled the conditions." "But how can I know when I receive the gift?" she queried. "Because it is quite safe to take Christ at His word."

Fenton Hall, the spirit-filled missionary who laid down his life in Amazonia, used to spend hours in prayer for this blessing. Yet in his innermost soul he knew that there was a life of greater liberty and joy and illumination of the Word than he had as yet received.

One day he had a conversation with a lady who pointed out a very simple promise in Luke 11:13: That our Heavenly Father gives the Holy Spirit to them that ask Him, and that one must be willing to accept the fullness of the Holy Spirit without any feeling whatever, just because God says so. She said that after she herself had done this, "only a few minutes elapsed when the word of God which had been in my mind became like a flame in my spirit."

That same night Fenton Hall fell on his knees, and fulfilled the conditions then and there by asking God to give him the fullness of the Holy Spirit, to do in his heart whatsoever He saw was necessary to meet his need. And God wonderfully answered that prayer, both by giving him a full assurance that He had heard his cry, and by marvelously opening up the Word of God. So markedly was his life changed and made more Christlike that another became hungry for the same blessing, until he, too, received it.

A fellow student said of Hall, "I think he was the greatest man I have ever met."

It may help some if we give here Fenton Hall's four rules of life.

1. Full submission to God: and a constant state of surrender.
2. A constant looking to God for guidance; and expecting Him to guide.
3. Acting in absolute obedience to such guidance.
4. A constant realization that of ourselves we can do nothing.

No wonder he wrote, "Praise God, it is all on the height just now, but sometimes it is higher heights than others." Then he added, "I suppose I am traveling up the stairway of Ephesians 3:14—21."

Yes—and what a wonderful stairway that is! Only the Holy Spirit can lead us up that way.

Shall we too claim the gift of Pentecost? God's invitation to every one of His followers is this: "Let him take hold of my strength" (Isa. 27:5).

> I take the promised Holy Ghost,
> I take the gift of Pentecost,
> To fill me to the uttermost;
> I take: He Undertakes.

7

How Does the Power Manifest Itself?

When "power from on high" comes down upon a believer how will it reveal itself? That is to say: What are the distinguishing marks of a Power-Full Christian?

Someone has put it very beautifully in this way: "He who has most of the Holy Spirit talks most about the Lord Jesus." Do we think much about Him? Do we talk much about Him?

Does not Paul himself say very much the same thing? "Be filled with the Spirit," he says, then he immediately goes on, "*speaking one to another* in psalms and hymns and spiritual songs, singing and making melody with your heart to the Lord" (Eph. 5:18–19). "They that feared the Lord spake often one to another" (Mal. 3:16). "They were all filled with the Holy Spirit and *began to speak. . . .*" (Acts 2:4). Unless we are willing to speak to one another and to tell "how great things the Lord hath done for us" we are not filled with the Holy Spirit and power.

In giving the Holy Spirit, God gives Himself; and He "cannot be hid." John the Baptist, the great forerunner of Christ, was filled with the Holy Spirit. What did he chiefly speak about? He had two great themes: "Behold the Lamb of God who taketh away the sin of the world" (John 1:29); and "He shall baptize you with the Holy Spirit and with fire" (Matt. 3:11). The Holy Spirit gives us "utterance" (Acts 2:4),; let us be willing to speak.

Many Christians have been bitterly disappointed because

they did not realize any great acquisition of "power" when they surrendered themselves fully to the Lord Jesus. They did not rise to high levels of service; they were not even conscious of any great spiritual uplift. They compared their experiences with others and were cast down in disappointment. They saw that others were far more successful than themselves, and were despondent.

Once again let us remind ourselves that we must not mark out any definite channel in which we think the blessing ought to flow. It is folly to attempt to guide or control or limit the Holy Spirit of God.

We must not expect Him to manifest Himself to us or through us, just in the same way as He manifested Himself in the lives of others we know.

There are some who seem to be expecting some mysterious thrill or electric shock instead of rivers of living water flowing out of their inmost being, to refresh the world. We must beware of limiting God.

He wants us to be "conformed" to the image of His Son"; not to the experience of some other Christian.

Let us not always be expecting to feel the Holy Spirit's power working in us. Paul said to the Corinthians, "I was with you in weakness, and in fear, and in much trembling. And my speech and my preaching was . . . in demonstration of the Spirit and of power" (1 Cor. 2:3−4). "When I am weak," says he, "then I am strong." He felt weak but he *was strong.* "Most gladly, therefore, will I rather glory in my weaknesses that the strength of Christ may rest upon me"— *cover* me, literally, "spread a tabernacle over me" (2 Cor. 12:9−10 RV).

To be "filled with the Spirit" is not necessarily having wonderful and uplifting feelings and thoughts of our Lord's great glory and goodness: but it is having Christ glorified *in me;* that is, in my life and by my lips. We ought to have "joy in the Holy Spirit", but He does not endue us with power just for our own enjoyment. One has aptly said, it is not to "feel like singing all the time", but to feel like *serving* all the time.

At a conference of Christian workers, one man declared

that he had been living on the Mount of Transfiguration for five weeks. "Wait a minute, brother," said Mr. Moody, who was presiding, "How many souls have been led to Christ in your ministry, in those five weeks?" "I hardly know," replied the man. "Do you know of any saved?" asked Mr. Moody again. "I am afraid not," was the answer. "Well," said the evangelist, "you are living too high up; no man ought to be so high as not to be able to reach souls."

Even when we cannot see or feel the least evidence of His working within, we are by faith to believe that He dwells in us and to count on His working out His purposes in and through us.

The children of Israel never once saw the Shekinah glory of the most holy place, yet all their actions and all their movements were influenced by it. And all their faith rested upon the indwelling Presence. At Pentecost the disciples were not told to be more earnest or more faithful; not to put forth more strenuous efforts. But they received the "life of Christ" in an entirely new way and made it visible to the world.

"The law of the Spirit of life in Christ Jesus" made them free from the law of sin and death (Rom. 8:2).

Remember that the evidence of the Holy Spirit's power is shown not by gifts but by fruit. "By their fruits ye shall know them." That is our Lord's test. What we *are* is far more important than what we *do*. The great work of the Holy Spirit is to make men *holy*—for without holiness no man can see the Lord; and we can only endure by seeing Him who is invisible.

Do not make the mistake of confusing "power from on high" with eloquence of speech, ability to teach, or skill in conducting the affairs of God in Sunday school, church, or parish—valuable as all these things are.

When Anskar went to Sweden as a pioneer missionary he told the natives that he had come from the great God. They at once replied, "Show us a miracle and we will believe you." He answered, "By the help of God I will show you the greatest of all miracles—*a holy life*. And that is only possible by the power of the Holy Spirit.

"Did you ever meet a Christian who strikes you at once as being Christ-like?" said a speaker recently. "It has a more powerful effect than the most eloquent sermon."

That is the manifestation of power from on high. When the life of Jesus is made manifest—visible—in our body (2 Cor. 4:11), then and then only is there power from on high.

If only every one of us would resolve with Paul, "Christ *shall be magnified in my body*" (Phil. 1:20), there would be no more complaints of "lack of power." "Not I, but Christ," must be the continual aim of every Power-Full Christian.

That was the "power" seen and felt in the Sadhu Sundar Singh. "He looks just like Jesus Christ," said one. "He stayed with us for three weeks," wrote a friend of the writer's, "and I never met anyone who reminded me so much of Jesus Christ." When we are bringing forth the fruit of the Spirit we can rely upon God to endow us with "gifts." We question whether it is right to seek any special gift of the Holy Spirit.

The word of wisdom, knowledge, faith, the gift of healing, the working of miracles ("powers"), prophecy, discerning of spirits, tongues and the interpretation of tongues—"all these [gifts] worketh that one and the self-same Spirit, dividing to every man severally as He will' (1 Cor. 12:7—11). And every man may confidently expect some "gift," for Paul, writing by the Holy Spirit, says, "The manifestation of the Spirit is given to every man" (v. 7).

We are all members of the body of Christ, but the body has many members; and all members have not the same office, and therefore do not all need the same gift. It is not necessary for the tongue to walk or the hand to speak. We can rely upon God to endue us with *power to do His will,* whatever His plan for us may be.

"God is able to make all grace about unto you; that ye, always having all sufficiency, may abound unto every good work" (2 Cor. 9:8) or, as Dr. Moffatt renders it: "so that you may always have quite enough for any emergency of your own and ample besides for any kind act to others."

Surely that statement is enough for every one of us. To all

who seek to be Power-Full Christians we would urge: Do not fix your mind on some coveted gift; but, keeping your eyes on Christ Jesus, allow the Holy Spirit to illuminate your heart and life and show you if in any place you are failing to bring forth the "fruit of the Spirit."

Weymouth says: "The Spirit . . . brings a harvest of love, joy, peace; patience towards other, kindness, benevolence; good-faith, meekness, self-restraint" (Gal. 5:22).

That is how the Holy Spirit manifests His presence. No one can "work up" these things. No one can force himself to love or be joyous or full of peace.

The Holy Spirit cannot possess us in all His fullness until we are willing to bring forth the fruit of the Spirit.

Are we showing forth *love?* Human love is very real; but Christian love is a manifestation of the love of God in and *through* the human heart. "The love of God, shed abroad in our hearts by the Holy Ghost" (Rom. 5:5). Who can measure the love of the Father for His only begotten Son Jesus Christ? *That is the love given us.* For our Lord prayed to the Father: "I made known unto them thy name . . . that the love wherewith thou lovedst me may be in them, and I in them" (John 17:26 RV). This is surely a special love, something even greater than His love to the world. We know that it is love "to the uttermost" (John 13:1 RV). That is the *love* the Holy Spirit brings into the heart if we allow Him to do so.

Is there *joy* in our lives? The joy which was in Christ remaining—abiding—in us making our joy full? (John 15:11). For joy is preeminently the fruit of the Spirit; "joy unspeakable and full of glory" (1 Peter 1:8). This, too, is power. St. Paul prays, "Now the God of Hope fill you with all joy and peace in believing, that ye may abound in hope, in the power of the Holy Ghost" (Rom. 15:13).

Truly "the joy of the Lord is your strength"—your stronghold (Neh. 8:10).

Is my life full of *peace?* A peace which passeth understanding? Twice on the day of His Resurrection the Lord Jesus said to His disciples, "Peace be unto you." Then He breathed on them and said, "Receive ye the Holy Ghost" (John 20:21–22).

It seems to me that we waste time seeking wondrous manifestations of the Holy Spirit or seeking to be filled with the Spirit, so long as we are deliberately grieving the Spirit by any unlove towards others; any murmuring or complaining; any unrest of soul. Let us see to it that we are wholeheartedly willing to allow the Holy Spirit to exhibit the fruit of the Spirit in our lives. When once we are fully yielded to Him, gladly, willingly surrendered to all His working— yes, even to that last virtue in the list given in Galatians 5:22–23, "self-restraint"—then the Holy Spirit can trust us with power.

We have already referred to the life of Ernest George Fenton Hall. In 1922 he won the officers' heavy-weight boxing championship in the Royal Air Force. After his conversion, he was, with others, running a Watch-Night service. A big crowd of roughians had gathered. An unwise worker laid a hand upon a lad who was blaspheming. The youth flew at the throat of this worker, who was in danger of being strangled.

Fenton Hall quickly stalked down the room, picked up the offending lad in his arms, and carried him out—the lad punching his face all the time. Someone foolishly closed the door behind Fenton Hall, leaving him outside, at the mercy of the crowd. They all set on him. Although his face was already badly battered by the indignant lad, Fenton Hall simply folded his arms and stood to his full height, 6' 4 1/2", with his back to the door and with a smile on his face. He bore the marks of the punishment they gave him for a long time. Someone, remembering his fame as a champion boxer, said to him, "Mr. Hall, did not you want to 'lay out' those fellows when they were attacking you?" He looked at his questioner with almost a puzzled expression and replied, "It never even entered my head!" Yet before his conversion he had a tremendously hot temper, and woe be to anyone who crossed him! But now his one aim was God's glory, and hence he could be trusted with power from on high. The fruit of the Spirit extends even to self-control—or rather Christ-control, for Fenton Hall was so yielded to Christ that the idea of "letting out" never even occurred to him!

How does the "power" manifest itself? Again we reply, chiefly in enabling us to bring forth the fruit of the Spirit. (Gal. 5:22). Such virtues cannot be produced by any effort on our part. They cannot, as we have said, be simulated or feigned or "worked up."

Spurgeon went so far as to say that we cannot promote the glory of God or bless the souls of others unless the Holy Spirit is in us in all His fullness. Then a man becomes indeed a burning and a shining light; burning within and shining without. The commonest bush becomes extraordinary when aflame with fire. Men will "turn aside to see" any man ablaze with God. Such a man will "speak fire-flames" as did the Apostles at Pentecost. The bush that attracted Moses's attention "burned with fire, and the bush was not consumed" (Exod. 3:2). Do you see what that meant? *None of the burning flames were due to the bush.* It was all of God and none of self. A bush which is itself burning makes much crackling, but attracts little attention. Let us, then, not look for any manifestation of the Spirit distinct from the fruit of the Spirit; the Spirit "of power, and of love and of a sound mind" (2 Tim. 1:7).

The "power" we seek is power to witness; converting power. In John 16 have you noticed the connection between verses 7 and 8? Our Lord says of the Holy Spirit, "I will send him unto you. And when he is come [to you], he will convict the world of sin, and of righteousness and of judgment." That conviction of sin can only come to the "world" when the Holy Spirit is dwelling in us believers in all His fullness. Our Lord said, "The Spirit of the Lord is upon me because he hath anointed me to preach glad tidings to the poor. . . ." And the same Holy Spirit desires to work in like manner through us.

The Spirit of the Lord will, both by our lives and lips, convince others of sin, and of righteousness and of judgment, when He is present in us in all His fullness. Our Lord came "to put away sin" (Heb. 7:26), and it was "through the

Eternal Spirit that he offered himself without spot unto God." In the same way, through the same Eternal Spirit, He will purge—cleanse—our conscience to serve the living God (v. 14).

When we have allowed the "Holy Spirit of promise" to enlighten our understanding, that we "may know what is the hope of his calling, and what the riches of the glory of his inheritance in the saints, . . . and what is the exceeding greatness of his power toward us who believe. . . ." (Eph. 1:13−19), then we can claim the "working of his mighty power," if we have allowed Him to "put away sin" in our lives, and cleanse our consciences.

Here again let us repeat that our consciences must be "void of offense both toward God and man."

When we can say with Paul: My conscience bears me witness in the Holy Ghost (Rom. 9:1), then the power can manifest itself.

The Power-Full Christian can be more easily recognized than described. People know intuitively when a person is filled with the Holy Spirit. Peter knew at once when the Spirit fell upon Cornelius and his household. Simon Magus recognized a difference in the Samaritans. He "saw" that the Holy Spirit was given (Acts 8:18). Paul seems to have detected at once that the Ephesian Christians had not received the Holy Spirit. He noticed there was something lacking (Acts 19:2).

When "the Spirit of the Lord God is upon us" men will see that the glory of the Lord is risen upon us (Isa. 60:1; 61:1).

The Holy Spirit glorifies Christ through us when we are content and desirous to let it be obvious that we are nothing in ourselves, but the Lord "has wrought all our works in us" (Isa. 26:12).

"Power from on high" is not a great increase of intellectual and moral power. It is much more than mere earnestness, zeal, reasoning skill or eloquence. It is not just persuasiveness, logic or lucidity, valuable as all these things seem to be. Herod could speak with the voice as of a god, yet his words were devoid of power. The "tongue of an archangel" is valueless without love. Some have thought that this power is the utterance of divine truth under the guidance and illumination of the Holy Spirit. But God can use a Power-Full Christian even when he is speechless! His life, and often his very looks are invested with power.

Music, art, and rhetoric may be used by God, but a man is useless to God unless that man is controlled by God's Holy Spirit. No natural, educational, intellectual, or moral gifts can take the place of "power from on high."

Many churches today are making the grievous mistake of relying upon pleasing architecture, sensuous and beautiful music, gorgeous vestments, wonderful ritual and imposing ceremonies, instead of claiming the power of the Holy Spirit. The plea is put forward that we must give God the best. He asks for ourselves; nothing less. It is the temple of our bodies that He desires to be beautiful and full of praise.

We set out to show *how* the power of God manifests itself. We must frankly confess that we cannot tell.

The Apostles received power at Pentecost. They were only "ignorant and unlearned men," their opponents said; but those enemies to the cause of Christ "were not able to resist the wisdom and the spirit by which they spake" (Acts 6:10).

Truly there is a fire that lies not in words or in tones, but which comes from the heart and is inflamed from above; a mysterious, irresistible fire which turns sinners into saints and compels saints to claim full sanctification.

We cannot adequately describe or define this power. Dr. Jowett said of Mr. Moody, "Moody's excellency was in an earthen vessel, and many Doctors of Divinity have wondered at the strange association. There were thousands of speakers more eloquent than Moody; and thousands of better singers than Sankey, whose lives were as chaste and striking; but the treasure was not there in overwhelming glory." Moody may have been uneducated, untutored, and unskilled in public speaking. But when he spoke, the power of an unseen world seemed to fall upon the audience.

Dr. Charles Inwood, writing recently from Denmark an account of a convention held there, said, "Messengers—message—people—were all alike under the mastery of the

Holy Spirit. Every sentence uttered seemed to possess a personality that reached and gripped the hearers."

It is just the manifested presence of Jesus Christ that is *power.* When Ignatius stood before his judges they said, "You are called the God-bearer; what mean you by this?" He replied, "I am a God-bearer: God dwells in me."

A man may have the learning of the wisest, and the eloquence of Demosthenes or Cicero. He will draw the crowds, but his message cannot be blessed without the Holy Spirit's unction. Many preachers are orthodox, but not Spirit-filled. And there is nothing more deadly than the Gospel without the Spirit's power. "The letter killeth, but the Spirit giveth life." Any man can be a powerful preacher if he will only yield himself unreservedly unto God. It will not matter in the very smallest degree whether a man is eloquent or whether he is not. Believe me, eloquence or learning have not the slightest influence on the power of our message. Every vestige of any power there may be in our words is due to the Holy Spirit of God. Nor is eloquence needed to draw a congregation.

During the East Anglican Revival, two or three years ago, crowds came together as if by magic. It was not advertisement or organization that accounted for the vast congregations. God's Holy Spirit was working through a wholly consecrated man.

Men and women were convicted of sin who had never come near the mission. The "power" is not limited. At Pentecost it filled not only the Upper Room, but *all the house.* Study the causes of any great revival and you will be amazed to find that God nearly always seems to use not the—so-called—great religious leaders, but invariably some devout layman or comparatively unknown minister.

It need not be so. But the fact remains that any true believer on the Lord Jesus may become a Power-Full Christian today. And then he becomes endued with a wonderful influence which draws men to God. His lips and his life make men hunger and thirst after righteousness.

As we have said before, although we cannot define this power, but it is not the less evident. Some months ago, a clergyman wrote me that a lady in his parish had told him that for years she had been praying for, and pleading with, her husband to accept Christ as his Savior, but in vain. He gave her a copy of *How to Live the Victorious Life.* Before the week was out she had won her husband. She read the book, yielded herself unconditionally to God, and then spoke to her husband. After his conversion he said to her, "Wife, why didn't you tell me these things before?" She replied, "I have been trying to do so for six years, without succeeding." Why, then, did she succeed now? Simply because she had received "power from on high."

Yes, the world soon recognizes the existence of God's power. Luther received power, and even his enemies admitted that he could obtain from God anything he asked! John Knox received power and Mary Queen of Scots often said she feared the prayers of that one man more than the fleets and armies of Queen Elizabeth.

A poorly educated working-lad of twenty years old received power, and wherever he goes today a little revival breaks out. William Hoste says, "A man full of the Spirit will be full of Christ." He will not be full of himself, nor will he *say* he is "full of the Spirit." Possibly he will not be aware of it. But others will "take knowledge of him."

"I hear you had a wonderful time at the mission last night?" said an interested inquirer. "Yes," was the answer, "and would you like to know the reason? It pleased the Holy Spirit to illuminate the face of Jesus Christ, and men saw and believed." That was the manifestation of power.

Many Christians, however, who have claimed the fullness of power are sometimes discouraged because they discover inconsistency in their own lives. Do we not, surely, expect the Holy Spirit to reveal our infirmities and also to show us the Lord Jesus as the Healer of those weaknesses?

We must not expect the Holy Spirit to work unnecessary miracles in us. Even after Pentecost the rulers perceived that the Apostles "were unlearned and ignorant men" from the world's standpoint. The Holy Spirit did not correct their Galilean speech. Nor did He take from Simon Peter his racial prejudices. At first, Peter had no love for the Gentiles; they were "common and unclean" (Acts 10:14), and he still retained his hatred for the Samaritans. He had no message for either of them, and no desire to go to them, although the Master had said, "Go ye into all the world and preach the Gospel." But God graciously gave him a vision on the housetop at Joppa. God showed him his error, and he immediately obeyed the call of God. "God hath shown me that I should not call any man common or unclean," said he (Acts 10:28).

We need not be distressed if God shows us sin in our life if only we are willing to have it put away *at once.*

Peter, as a Jew, hated the Samaritans. A Jew would not even show a lost Samaritan the way, or point a thirsty one to a well! But the Christian brotherhood sent Simon Peter to see if Samaria had indeed "received the Word of God." And behold! The Holy Spirit fell upon Samaritans even in the city of Ahab and Jezebel!

Philip, *a deacon,* was chosen to "serve table" (Acts 6:2– 5), while the Apostles gave themselves "continually to prayer and to the ministry of the word." "Full of faith and of the Holy Spirit," Philip was preaching the Word both at Samaria and Caesarea long before the Apostle Peter arrived (Acts 8:5, 12–13, 40).

We often see this today. Business men (Acts 6:3) are often filled with the Holy Spirit and start a great spiritual work while we clergy hold back! How wonderfully Philip the deacon was led by the Holy Spirit!

Then differences of opinion may arise between two Spirit-filled men. Who has not seen it? The Holy Spirit is "the bond of peace," and we are to "endeavor to keep the unity of the Spirit" (Eph. 3:4). Yet we read that although the Holy Spirit said, "Separate Me Barnabas and Saul for the work where-unto I have called them" (Acts 13:2), these two men soon "contended" with one another so sharply "that they parted asunder the one from the other" (Acts 15:39).

Later on we find Paul upbraiding Simon Peter face to face "because he was to be blamed" (Gal. 2:11).

Such dissensions are not the manifestation of the Holy

Spirit, but they show us how careful and prayerful we must be, even if the Holy Spirit comes to us in all His fullness.

We need say no more upon how the Spirit manifests Himself in men's lives; but let us pray much. There are so many among us who have remarkable gifts but lack of fullness of power. Two Spirit-filled evangelists were speaking about one of the most able Bible teachers in America, so far as mere teaching was concerned, a man wonderfully knowledgable in the Scriptures. "Yes," said one, a little sadly, "that man just needs one thing: the touch of the Spirit of God." Have we received that "touch"? God alone knows what a transformation it would make in our lives, our message, our mission and our influence.

The most able Bible teacher, or the untutored African, or the godly Professor of Divinity is alike transfigured and empowered by it. When Bishop Moule was a Professor of Divinity at Cambridge he received that "touch." Scholarly, cultured, refined to the Nth degree, he recognized the change that came over him. He says, "When I secured a more intelligent and conscious hold upon the living and most gracious personality of the Holy Spirit, it was a new development of insight into the love of God. It was a new contact, as it were, with the inner and eternal movements of redeeming goodness and power, a new discovery of Divine resources."

The Holy Spirit desires to "clothe Himself" with us as He did with Gideon. He would think through our minds, look out of our eyes, speak through our voice, work with our hands. "The miracle of Gideon anticipates the Incarnation," says the writer, "and the miracle of Pentecost perpetuates it."

All he asks is that He may possess us wholly; anyone of us, everyone of us.

Early in 1924 a missionary traveling in Liberia discovered isolated groups of Christians eager for teachers. He found no fewer than 150 churches, each with a big Bible which no one could read—obtained through traders; and literally thousands of natives longing to know more about the true God. On one occasion this missionary had a congregation of

12,000. How did this happen? Some years ago a Krooman native, who called himself William Harris, went to Lagos as a laborer. He was converted there, and *claimed the fullness of the Holy Spirit*. He went back to his own people on fire for Christ. His burning words led them to cast away their fetishes, idols and charms and to abandon their juju worship of thousands of years. Witchcraft and cannibalism were given up wherever he went. He moved through the country, saying that another would follow him who would teach them! The missionary in his journey enrolled 21,900 catechumens. The "power of the Holy Spirit" does what nothing else can do.

A slave boy in the hinterland of West Africa runs away because of the brutal treatment, and finds his way to the coast, where he hears of God. He sees a lad from his own tribe praying. "What are you doing?" "Talking to God." "Who is God?" asked Sammy. "He is my Father," answered the lad. "Then you are talking to your Father."

Henceforth Sammy Morris, as they had nicknamed him, regarded God as *his Father*. Sammy "talked" to him. Ignorant, unlettered, destitute of religion, yet his cry—his talk—was heard by God. He obtained forgiveness and yielded himself in simple faith utterly to his Father. And God, always true to His word, guided him and provided for him. A lady missionary told him about the Holy Spirit. He longs to know more. "If you want to know any more you must go to Stephen Merritt, of New York. He told me all I know of the Holy Spirit." "I am going," he said, calmly. The missionary laughed, and pointed out difficulties: but Sammy went.

He persuaded a blasphemous and brutal captain to let him work his passage on a sailing ship. His sweet assurance and unruffled peace while being slapped, cursed at, and kicked led to the conversion of the captain and many of the crew.

That ungainly lad, whose photo the writer has seen, was full of the Holy Spirit and power. He finds Mr. Merritt in New York. "I am Sammy Morris. I've just come from Africa to talk with you about the Holy Spirit," he said. That very evening he was left in the mission and forgotten. When Mr. Merritt sought him at 10:30 p.m. he found him surrounded by seventeen tramps on their faces in prayer. Sammy had pointed them to Christ! They were rejoicing in His pardoning favor.

Mr. Merritt says, "I had never seen such a sight. The Holy Spirit was in this figure of ebony; an uncultured, uncouth, uncultivated African, under the power of the Holy Spirit, the first night in America, winning souls for Immanuel, nearly a score."

Mr. Merritt took him in his coach to a funeral, and on the way began to point out the sights. "That's the Grand Opera House—" "Stephen Merritt," said Sammy, "do you ever pray in a coach?" "Yes, very often." "He placed his great black hand on mine," said Mr. Merritt, "and, turning me round on my knees, said, 'We will pray.' And, for the first time I knelt in a coach to pray. He told the Holy Spirit that he had come from Africa to talk to me about *Him*, and I talked about everything else, when he was so anxious to hear and know about *Him*; and he asked Him if He would not take out of my heart such things, and so fill me with Himself that I would never preach or write or talk but of Him. Never have I know such a day. We were filled with the Holy Spirit."

When people heard about Sammy many wrote for a photo. On seeing it for the first time Sammy exclaimed, "My picture is too ugly; oh, that I could send them a picture of Jesus!"

Yet that lad was filled with the Holy Spirit and with fire. The late Charles Alexander said, "I heard Stephen Merritt tell his experience with this humble boy. I have heard and forgotten hundreds of stories; but this one stays. Every remembrance of it uplifts and sweetens my work." That story is, indeed, a benediction.

But the blessed Holy Spirit desires so to bless *us* and make *us* a blessing. Let us not fail Him and disappoint Him.

8
How to Increase the Blessing

We are to grow in grace. So then, it is not a question of how to maintain the blessing, but how to increase it. We need to know how to "abide in Christ," how to "walk by the Spirit," so as to "be strengthened with power through his Spirit in the inner man" (Eph. 3:16 RV).

There is a glorious and "perfect freedom," together with increasing blessedness and power, for those who obey the law of the Spirit and His law is all grace! For "the law of the Spirit is life in Christ Jesus" (Rom. 8:2).

There are men living today who were once mightily used of God who have now become "castaway," rejected; not lost, but put aside as unfit for service (1 Cor. 9:27). And this, not because of some shameful fall or grave betrayal of trust, but simply because they neglected to keep themselves in the love of God. Others are rejected in the counsels of God, but are still working as strenuously as ever, though fruitlessly. They, like Samson of old, did not know that the Lord's power had departed from them, so they go out and shake themselves as at other times (Judges 16:20). But nothing happens. Why is this? It is because they neglected one of three things. Of these we wish to speak, for every one of us must beware lest a worse thing befall us. "Let him that thinketh he standeth take heed lest he fall."

We cannot stand still; either we go on "from strength to strength" until we appear before God (Ps. 84:7), or we go back, growing weaker and more powerless.

But if we are careful to observe these things we shall assuredly increase in spiritual stature and power. There stands first of all.

1. *Obedience.* Simon Peter, who once dared to say to His blessed Master, "Be it far from thee!"; and who even said, "Not so, Lord!" after being filled with the Holy Spirit at Pentecost came to learn that the path of obedience is the only pathway to blessing. It is Simon who said that God gives the Holy Spirit to them that obey Him (Acts 5:32).

Have you noticed that, almost in the same breath, our Lord, three times over, couples together love and obedience and the sure blessing that follows them? It is very striking. (1) "If ye love me, keep my commandments. And I will pray the Father, and he shall give you another Comforter, that he may abide with you for ever . . . the Spirit of Truth . . . He dwelleth with you and shall be in you" (John 14:15−17).

(2) "He that hath my commandments, and keepeth them, he it is that loveth me: and he that loveth me shall be loved of my Father, and I will love him, and will manifest myself [the Son] to him" (v. 21).

(3) "If a man love me, he will keep my words: and my Father will love him and we will come unto him, and make our abode with him." (v. 23).

Here is a marvelous threefold cord which binds us with silken and welcome bonds to our Triune God.

His commandments obeyed with a loving heart bring a threefold blessing. (1) The abiding Holy Spirit (v. 16). (2) The manifestation of Christ our Lord (v. 21). (3) The manifestation of the Father; and the permanent abiding of the Father and the Son with the believer (v. 23). Can we ask for more than this? No blessing can exceed these. And it is only in this way that we can "be to the praise of the glory" of the Father (Eph. 1:3, 5): and to the praise of the glory of the Son (vv. 10 and 12): and to the praise of the glory of the Holy Spirit (vv. 13−14).

What a calling! What a privilege!—to everyone who has learned "to trust and obey." With what joy we would study the Holy Bible if we understood this, and realized what it meant. How eagerly we should search His Word to find out

His commandments, His will for us! The Power-Full Christian is one whose delight is in the law of the Lord; and in His law doth he meditate day and night (Ps. 1:2).

Is it not amazing that anyone who knows the love of Jesus for what it is, should ever hesitate to obey Him?

"Christ became obedient unto death, even the death of the Cross. Wherefore God hath highly exalted him," says Paul, when challenging believers to obey. Was not obedience the basis of our Christ's earthly life? His life's motto was this: "When He cometh into the world he saith . . . 'Lo, I am come (in the volume of the book it is written of me,) to do thy will, O God' " (Heb. 10:5−7 RV).

We also must follow in His steps, and obey. "For it is God which worketh in you both to will and to do of his good pleasure" (Phil. 2:8-13).

Remember there is no blessing, no power apart from obedience. With willingness and readiness to obey come power, for then *God* works in us, instead of the "spirit that now worketh in the children of disobedience" (Eph. 2:2).

The manifestation of Christ always comes to those who lovingly obey. As when we received the Spirit so let us walk in the Spirit, keeping ourselves in the love of God (Jude 21).

Holiness is simply obedience to God in all the details of life. In little things as well as great ones, the Holy Spirit desires to control us, and to guide us. All the manifold details of the home life; all the perplexities of our business life; all the problems of our social life; all the questionings of our hearts the Holy Spirit is wishful to decide and to answer.

When the Spirit is truly Lord of our life there is perfect peace and rest. This means a spirit of recollectedness on our part. We shall cease to get excited, or hurried or worried. We shall speak and act and work quietly. And whenever the spirit which is in the world steals in and interrupts our communion and our trust we shall "recall ourselves quietly into the presence of God" as Fenelon counsels us to do. Our words will be fewer, but more effectual. We may seem to do less, but all we do will be more profitable.

We shall "study to be quiet" (1 Thess. 4:11). We shall learn by blessed experience what that saying means, "He that believeth shall not make haste."

"Be still and know that I am God." "For thus saith the Lord God, the Holy One . . . in quietness and confidence shall be your strength" (Isa. 30:15). Can there be any confidence greater than that produced by the knowledge that the Lord God Almighty is with us to take over for us? "We know that all things work together for good to them that love God" (Rom. 8:28).

A man who had just yielded Himself to God, turning from darkness to light, said, "I am going to do the will of God today, without thinking of tomorrow." Years afterwards he testified that this simple decision brought him unspeakable blessing.

Dr. Wilbur Chapman met General Booth and asked him what was the secret of his success. His reply is noteworthy. "I will tell you the secret," he said. "God has had all there was of me. There have been many men with greater brains than I, and men with greater opportunities; but from the day that I got the poor of London on my heart, and a vision of what Christ could do for them, I made up my mind that God should have all there was of William Booth. And if there is anything of power in my work it is because God has all the love of my heart, all the power of my will, and all the influence of my life."

Fellow-Christian, what would happen if you believed God?

But you ask: How does the Spirit guide? How does He speak to us? He speaks through conscience, and he speaks through the lives and lips of others; but He speaks very specially through the Holy Scriptures. And that is the second thing to be careful about.

To increase the blessing we must

2. *Study our Bible.* Surely this is self-obvious. For, to put it very bluntly, if the Holy Spirit is to work in me, I *must allow Him to do His work.*

What is that? Our Lord said, "He shall glorify me: for he shall take of mine and shall declare it unto you" (John 16:14 RV). The Holy Spirit does not speak of Himself; He takes the words of Christ, and illuminates them, and shows them unto us. Now the Bible is full of Christ Jesus.

Thus, to allow the Holy Spirit to work powerfully, we must be men of the Word. For the Bible is the work of the Holy Spirit. It is His language.

When the writer of the Epistle to the Hebrews quotes Psalm 95 he says it is the Holy Spirit speaking. Wherefore even as the Holy Spirit saith, "Today, if ye will hear his voice, harden not your hearts" (Heb. 3:7–8 rv). A hardened heart is a powerless heart. "All Scripture is given by inspiration of God" (2 Tim. 3:16).

In the Scriptures "holy men of God spake as they were moved by the Holy Spirit" (2 Peter 1:21). The Bible is the voice of God. Hear it. Read it. For our Lord especially favors and blesses and works through those who receive and obey His word. "To this man will I look; even to him that is poor and of a contrite heart and trembleth at My word" (Isa. 66:2).

Do we desire sanctification? Then remember that we are sanctified by the Word of Truth (John 17:17). Did not our Lord Himself say, "The words that I have spoken unto you are spirit, and are life" (John 6:63 rv)? Our Lord's first care after His resurrection was not to tell of the glories of heaven, but to "open the Scriptures" to His disciples, and to open "their understanding that they might understand the Scriptures" (Luke 24:32–45).

The self-same Holy Spirit desires today to open our hearts to give heed to the things spoken of God, as He did for Lydia (Acts 16:14). The only way to understand God's dealings with us is to know the Scriptures. If Peter had not been familiar with the teaching of the Prophets, how could he have cried so confidently at Pentecost, "This is that which was spoken by the prophet Joel"? (Acts 2:16).

The Holy Spirit first gave the Word and only the Holy Spirit can interpret that Word to us.

We "know all things through the Spirit." "No man can say that Jesus is Lord, but in the Holy Ghost" (1 Cor. 12:3).

And no man, however vast his scholarship, can understand the deeper truths of God as revealed in Scriptures, save by the Holy Spirit's help.

The scholars' "findings" (so-called) are often losings. We must "have the mind of Christ" to understand the Bible.

"We speak," says Paul, "not in words which man's wisdom teacheth, but which the Holy Ghost teacheth" (1 Cor. 2:13).

"In the wisdom of God, the world by wisdom knew not God" (1 Cor. 1:21). Scholarship is invaluable when Spirit-taught, but a snare and a delusion otherwise.

The Power-Full Christian, however, is one who is able to say with the Apostle, "My speech and my preaching were not in persuasive words of wisdom, but in demonstration of the Spirit and of power" (1 Cor. 2:4 RV).

The Word of God is the sword of the Spirit (Eph. 6:17), who dwells within us: let us see to it that we do not leave Him to fight our battles without that sword. But a "sword" requires a Hand to wield it and so the Bible is not effective apart from the Holy Spirit.

It was the Holy Spirit who spake through Paul when he said, "Take the sword!" "Take . . . the sword of the Spirit, which is the Word of God" (Eph. 6:17). It is the Spirit's sword for He made it. He alone can put the edge on it. He only can use it and instruct us in its use. Beloved, obey the Holy Spirit's command. Take the sword! Remember that soldiers are not allowed to choose their own weapons. The Word of God is not only for our "comfort" (Rom. 15:4), and for our help in witnessing, but also for our defense against our spiritual enemy.

When our Lord was tempted by Satan in the wilderness, He "took the sword," although He had only the Old Testament Scriptures. Yet He might have chosen many other weapons, or He might have uttered some new word of power. Yet He "took the sword." So must we.

Our souls must be fed to be strong. And "man shall not live by bread alone, but by every word that proceedeth out of the mouth of God" (Matt. 4:4).

Last of all, we must be much in prayer.

3. *Prayer.* In the Scriptures God speaks to us, and we love to keep His commandments. In prayer we speak to God as

well as listen to His voice. And God loves to have our communion with Him. Just as we cannot understand the Bible without the teaching and illumination of the Holy Spirit, so we cannot pray without His help.

That was a touching revelation of the Father's loving care which our Lord gave to the poor, sinful woman at Samaria's well. He said that "true worshipers shall worship the Father in spirit and in truth," for, He adds, "the Father seeketh such to be his worshipers" (John 4:23 RV).

Every time we pray let us recollect that we are coming to a Father, who is seeking our prayer and our worship!

No Christian can be a Power-Full Christian unless he spends much time in prayer. A Christian is never so power-full as when he is praying; and the source of all prayer is the Holy Spirit of God. Our Lord Himself has chosen prayer as His great work in heaven. "He ever liveth to make intercession" for us (Heb. 7:25).

We must owe much—all?—to our Lord's intercession; for we are told that it is through it that He is "able to save to the uttermost." And it is just this "uttermost salvation" every one of us desires.

What does He pray for? We are not told. We know that before Peter's denial our Lord said, "I have prayed for thee, that thy faith fail not" (Luke 22:32). His prayers are very personal and very definite. Our Lord also promised, "I will pray the Father and he shall give you another Comforter" (John 14:16).

Then He also prayed, "Holy Father, keep them in thy name" (John 17:11 RV). And that is what we need every moment: to be "kept" abiding in Christ.

Here we need not talk much about prayer; that was spoken of in *The Kneeling Christian*. Is it not necessary or right for us to pray, "Take not Thy Holy Spirit from us"? We may, perhaps, pray this prayer in the congregation where many are as yet without Christ, for our prayers there are "common prayer"; that is, prayer for all.

The Holy Spirit has come to abide with us—in us—for ever (John 14:16–17). It was King David who offered up that cry, "Take not thy Holy Spirit from me" (Ps. 51:11). And we can see why he so prayed. Everyone knew that Saul was once "among the prophets." "The Spirit of the Lord came upon him" (1 Sam. 10:6, 10). But he—the anointed one—grievously sinned. He was rejected of God. God's Holy Spirit deserted him and evil spirits troubled him. So David, a youth of God, came to play the harp before the stricken king. David never forgot that sad experience, and in later years when he too sinned greviously he cried out, "Take not thy Holy Spirit from me" (Ps. 51:11)

But you and I need never utter such a prayer. We can "resist the Spirit," "grieve" the Spirit, and so "quench" the Spirit that He cannot work through us; but He came to abide with us for ever.

To remain full of the Holy Spirit, then, we must be full of prayer, for is He not "the Spirit of grace and supplication" (Zech. 12:10)?

If our prayers are to be heard we must "pray in the Spirit" (Jude 20)—that is, by the inspiration and in the power of the Spirit.

Prayer is the creation of the Holy Spirit. And the only prayers that God is bound to answer are those which the Holy Spirit inspires. Our prayers are a sure indication of our power. When the heart feels cold and unresponsive, let us not cease praying. For then is the time we need to pray most. Listen once more to the Holy Spirit's message to us through His servant, Paul, "In like manner the Spirit also helpeth our infirmity: for we know not how to pray as we ought; but the Spirit Himself maketh intercession for us with groanings which cannot be uttered; and He that searcheth the hearts knoweth what is the mind of the Spirit, because He maketh intercession for the saints, according to the will of God" (Rom. 8:26−27).

The Holy Spirit implants in us the desire to pray: teaches us what to pray for: and Himself prays for us.

Nothing is made more easy for us than prayer, if indeed we are "led by the Spirit." And the Holy Spirit's intercessions within us are sure and certain and powerful and divine as the Son's intercession at the right hand of God.

It is through the Holy Spirit that our bodies become

temples of the Holy Spirit, and that we are made "very members of Christ." But those temples must not be desecrated by being preoccupied by worldly things, or the Holy Spirit may need to take a "scourge of small cords" and drive out such buyers and sellers from His temple, so that it can, indeed, be a "house of prayer." For the body may be on its knees while the soul is far away from the mercy seat and our prayers are mere words. It is an awful thing to think that we can increase our sins by insincere "prayer." We must, indeed, pray "in spirit and in truth." We must really mean what we say and earnestly desire what we ask for.

A desire to obey God at all costs is magnificent. The Word of God, the sword of the Spirit, is all-powerful. But going forth to fight, even with the "whole armor of God" is not enough. We depend upon prayer.

Finally, brethren, be strong in the Lord and in the power of His might. Put on the whole armor of God . . . and having done all, stand. . . . Praying always with all prayer and supplication in the Spirit" (Eph. 6:10–18).

The Lord is at hand.